The Kitchen Ice Cream Cookbook

90+ Delicious & Easy-to-Make Ice Cream, Frozen Yogurt, Gelato & Sherbet Recipes your Family Will Enjoy

Written By
Wilson K. Lee

©Copyright 2020 by Wilson K. Lee - All rights reserved.

This document is geared towards providing exact and reliable information in regards to the topic and issue covered. The publication is sold with the idea that the publisher is not required to render accounting, officially permitted, or otherwise, qualified services. If advice is necessary, legal or professional, a practiced individual in the profession should be ordered.

From a Declaration of Principles which was accepted and approved equally by a Committee of the American Bar Association and a Committee of Publishers and Associations.

In no way is it legal to reproduce, duplicate, or transmit any part of this document in either electronic means or in printed format. Recording of this publication is strictly prohibited and any storage of this document is not allowed unless with written permission from the publisher. All rights reserved.

The information provided herein is stated to be truthful and consistent, in that any liability, in terms of inattention or otherwise, by any usage or abuse of any policies, processes, or directions contained within is the solitary and utter responsibility of the recipient reader. Under no circumstances will any legal responsibility or blame be held against the publisher for any reparation, damages, or monetary loss due to the information herein, either directly or indirectly.

Respective authors own all copyrights not held by the publisher.

The information herein is offered for informational purposes solely, and is universal as so. The presentation of the information is without contract or any type of guarantee assurance.

The trademarks that are used are without any consent, and the publication of the trademark is without permission or backing by the trademark owner. All trademarks and brands within this book are for clarifying purposes only and are the owned by the owners themselves, not affiliated with this document.

Contents

Introduction 1

Chapter 1 - Custard & Ice cream Recipes....................... 7

    Traditional Vanilla Custard.................................... 7

    Chocolate Pistachio Frozen Custard...................... 10

    Strawberry Custard Ice Cream................................13

    Lemon Pie Custard Ice Cream 16

    Blueberry Custard Ice Cream.................................19

    Frozen Banana Custard with Waffles..................... 22

    Coffee Custard Chocolate Ice Cream 25

    Mango Chia Seed Custard Ice Cream 28

    Avocado Pistachio Custard Ice Cream 31

    Toasted Black Sesame Ice Cream 34

Chapter 2 - Frozen Yogurt Recipes 37

    Coconut Strawberry Frozen Yogurt...................... 37

    Chunky Blackberry Frozen Yogurt 40

    Coconut Vanilla Frozen Yogurt............................. 42

    Hazelnut Chocolate Frozen Yogurt 45

    Leche Frozen Coconut Yogurt................................48

    Minty Blueberry Frozen Yogurt............................ 50

    Chocolate Raspberry Frozen Yogurt..................... 53

Instant Chocolate Chip Frozen Yogurt 55

Peanut Butter Frozen Yogurt.....................................58

Almond Hash Frozen Yogurt..................................... 61

Frozen Yogurt with Black Sesame.............................64

Matcha & Coconut Frozen Yogurt............................66

Maple Tahini Frozen Yogurt................................... 68

2 Berries Frozen Yogurt..70

Peach Frozen Yogurt with Nuts................................73

Mango Frozen Yogurt with Nuts...............................76

Kiwi Frozen Yogurt with Berries..............................78

Cantaloupe Frozen Yogurt...................................... 80

Avocado Frozen Yogurt... 82

Coconut Almond Frozen Yogurt............................... 84

Chocolate Chip Frozen Yogurt 86

Coconut Cashew Frozen Yogurt 88

Chapter 3 - Gelato Recipes..................................... 91

Simple Berry Gelato 91

Strawberry Homemade Gelato.................................94

Lemon Gelato 97

Stracciatella Gelato 100

Chocolate-Hazelnut Gelato....................................103

Chocolate Gelato 106

Smores Gelato with Nutella 109

Avocado gelato 112

Pistachio Gelato 115

Vanilla Cappuccino Gelato 118

Yogurt Gelato 121

Creamy Basil Gelato 124

Cinnamon Gelato 127

Sour Cream Gelato.. 130

Mango Gelato 133

Vegan Mango Gelato 136

Vegan Coffee Gelato 139

Vegan Chocolate Gelato 142

Vegan Maple Vanilla Gelato.. 145

Chapter 4 - Delicious Sherbet Recipes 148

Coconut Orange Sherbet 148

Coconut Lime Sherbet.. 151

Peach Sherbet with Cherries 153

Strawberry Coconut Sherbet... 156

Lemon Buttermilk Sherbet 159

Coconut Pineapple Sherbet... 162

Cocoa Cherry Sherbet.. 165

Avocado-Basil Sherbet 168

Cantaloupe Sherbet...171

Simple Banana Sherbet.. 174

Coconut Chocolate Sorbet 177

Creamy Mint Sherbet...180

Greek Yogurt & Chia Sherbet 183

Coconut Milk Orange Sherbet.............................186

Mango Buttermilk Sherbet 189

Avocado Sorbet...192

Blueberry Buttermilk Sherbet 195

Coconut Green Apple Sorbet............................... 197

Coconut Cranberries Sherbet 200

Melon Sherbet 203

Chapter 5 - Low Carb Ice cream Recipes 205

Low Carb Chocolate Chip Ice Cream 205

Low Carb Vanilla Ice Cream.............................. 209

Raspberry Rich Chocolate Ice Cream 212

Oreo Ice Cream.. 215

Cheesecake Ice Cream..218

Blackberry Buttermilk Ice Cream 220

Quick Coffee Ice Cream 223

Ice Cream with Chocolate Flake.........................225

Mint Chocolate Chip Ice Cream 228

Coconut Chip Ice Cream.. 231

Cinnamon Ice Cream...234

Coconut Caramel Ice Cream 237

Peanut Butter Ice Cream...240

Almond Butter Ice Cream 243

Pumpkin Ice Cream...246

Cashew Butter Ice Cream..249

Avocado Cream Cheese Ice Cream 252

Lemon Curd Pie Ice Cream 255

Strawberry Cheesecake Ice cream 258

Keto Coconut Ice Cream.. 261

Chapter 6 - Granita Recipes...264

Watermelon Granita..264

Mango-Lime Granita... 267

Fresh Strawberry Granita 270

Mint Avocado Granita 273

Coconut Raspberry Granita 276

CALORIES IN FOOD: CALORIE CHART DATABASE 279

COOKING MEASUREMENT (CONVERSIONS) 282

CONCLUSION 285

The Home Kitchen Ice Cream Cookbook

Introduction

Welcome! Look no further, this is the ultimate ice cream cookbook with over 90 custard, frozen yogurt, gelato, sherbet, and granita recipes to choose from. I hope you're excited to create and enjoy lots of delicious frozen desserts!

All these treats are super easy to churn out, with no ice cream machine necessary, making this a fun and exciting activity for the whole family. Who wouldn't love weekly homemade ice cream night?!

Every recipe can also be customized or personalized to your flavor preferences or dietary needs. No more endlessly scouring grocery store aisles for vegan or keto options! Gone are the days of unknown ingredients and harmful preservatives – now you know exactly what goes into your favorite sweet treats.

With recipes so simple, you probably have the ingredients already in your kitchen! Use organic, premium ingredients or incorporate fresh fruit from your garden for the true gourmet experience. Homemade ice cream is certainly the way to go for the freshest taste and peace of mind. WARNING: if you're not careful you might just become the next Ben or Jerry!

Before we start churning let's learn a bit more about what makes homemade ice cream so special.

1

Wilson K. Lee

Benefits of Homemade Ice Cream

Health

- Homemade ice cream is huge source of vitamins A, B-6, B-12, C, D, and E!
- Dairy contains important minerals like calcium and phosphorus
- It's also rich in carbohydrates, fats, and proteins, that are needed to provide energy to our body.
- Store brought ice cream is high in sugar and unhealthy chemicals. At home, you get to decide all the quantities and ingredients.

Freedom

- You can replace sugar with honey, fruits or sugar free sweeteners you may have around the kitchen.
- The flavor possibilities are endless! Use fresh ingredients to really taste a difference.
- You can make low calories, low carbs, and sugar free, dairy free ice cream according to your desired diet plan.

Convenience

- To make simple homemade ice cream you only need whole milk, eggs, sugar, vanilla extract, and heavy cream. These ingredients are likely already available in your kitchen!

- With most of these recipes, no ice cream machine required!
- Makes for a great inexpensive rainy day activity with family and friends.

I fell in love with homemade ice cream years ago. I was so passionate about finding the perfect consistency and new unique flavor combinations and it turns out, other people were too! I saw the huge demand for fresh, authentic sweet treats and I opened my own ice cream shop, 720 Sweets. Over time our business grew and grew and we were able to open a total of 7 worldwide locations!

Since then I've been super passionate about sharing my expertise and knowledge with new food business owners and ice cream lovers alike. If you're interested in learning more about turning your new favorite hobby into extra cash in your pocket I've included some resources in the Conclusion.

Now back to the ice cream! Here are the most common issues with homemade ice cream and my expert tips & tricks on how to solve them for the best possible results:

Common Homemade Ice Cream Mistakes

Too Hard or Soft

Nothing is more frustrating than dipping into rock hard ice cream. The culprit is usually low fat or sugar content. Sugar

Wilson K. Lee

decreases the freezing temperature of liquids and fat doesn't freeze. Up quantities of both to keep your ice cream soft and smooth. Alternatively, add in more salt, or some alcohol for the same effect. On the other hand, reduce quantities of these ingredients if the consistency is too soft.

Tastes like Artificial Candy

The whole point of homemade ice cream is the natural, rich flavor. If your product tastes like artificial candy, it's likely because the skimmed milk has been overheated. In the future go slow and steady with the heat when cooking your base.

Too Greasy

Ice cream is all about balance. While you may think that adding more dairy will up the creaminess, too much cream, buttermilk and milk content can leave your with a greasy texture. Everything in moderation!

Too Watery

Watery ice cream can be very disappointing. If you wanted a popsicle, you would've made that instead! Add in more dairy, fruits or experiment with other stabilizers to avoid this fate.

The Home Kitchen Ice Cream Cookbook

Melts Too Quickly

Homemade ice cream often melts very quickly because it contains less fat and air as compared to store bought alternatives. While this does provide some health benefits, it can be frustrating on a warm day. Either up your fat content or freezer temperature for a quick fix.

Tips & Tricks for Your Best Batch

- Freeze the ice cream container for at least 24 hours beforehand for faster setting time and solid results.
- Grind solid and coarse sweeteners in a spice grinder or food processor to avoid potential grainy textures.
- Add eggs yolks or a vegan alternative like avocado to make ice cream extra creamy.
- Never churn the ice cream near to kitchen, stove, oven, crockpot or other heat source!
- You want your ice cream base at the perfect temperature. I pour mine into an old quart-sized yogurt container and chill it in the fridge overnight.
- Only fill the ice cream container 1/2 or 1/3 full for best results since it will expand.
- When necessary, add eggs yolks slowly into the milk mixture to make sure they're fully incorporated.

Wilson K. Lee

- Wait to add flavor extracts until after the batter is cooled for accurate taste testing.
- Fold mix-ins, such as chocolate chips, nuts, etc. just once ice cream is ready.
- Homemade ice creams only keep well in the freeze for 1 week before they begin to lose their flavor and creamy texture.

Believe it or not, that's about all there is to it! Amazing what you can do with just a few ingredients and some love, isn't it? Now that you know all the common mistakes to avoid, homemade ice cream benefits, and expert tips & tricks you're all set up for sweet success. Happy Churning!

Chapter 1 - Custard & Ice cream Recipes

Traditional Vanilla Custard

You can't beat the classics! This custard uses egg yolks for a smoother, creamier texture than regular ice cream. With just 5 ingredients, you can feel confident that you're only serving the good stuff. Better still: no ice cream machine needed!

Wilson K. Lee

Prep Time   10Min

Cooking time   20 Min

Total Time   30 Min

Servings   6 servings

Equipment

Cooking pan

Ice cream maker optional

Ice cream container

INGREDIENTS

- 2 cups heavy whipped cream
- 1 cup whole milk
- ⅔ cup sugar
- ⅛ teaspoon fine sea salt
- 6 large egg yolks

DIRECTIONS

1. Heat a heavy bottom pot over medium heat.

The Home Kitchen Ice Cream Cookbook

2. Add heavy cream, milk, sugar and salt in pot and simmer for 5-10 minutes until all ingredients are well incorporated.
3. Remove pan from stove and let chill to room temperature.
4. Beat egg yolks in mixing bowl for 2-3 minutes. Slowly add cream mixture and beat again.
5. Add yolk mixture back to pan.
6. Cook mixture over medium to low heat and stir continuously, until yolk and cream mixture is thick.
7. Strain mixture through strainer in small bowl.
8. Let custard cool to room temperature.
9. If you are making ice cream without an ice cream machine, freeze ice cream container for 24 hours beforehand.
10. Pour mixture in container and chill at least 6 hours or overnight to set.
11. Alternatively,, churn mixture in an ice cream machine according to manufacturers' instructions.
12. Serve and enjoy!

NUTRITIONAL INFORMATION

Calories Per Servings, 273 kcal, 20.56 g Fat, 18.12 g Total Carbs, 4.72 g Protein, 0 g Fiber

Wilson K. Lee

Chocolate Pistachio Frozen Custard

Rich cocoa + nutty pistachios = a match made in heaven. Your kids will love the chocolate taste, and their bodies will love the nut's nutritional healthy fats, fiber, and protein. Once again – no expensive ice cream machine necessary!

Prep Time   10 Min

Cooking Time 25 Min

Total Time   35 Min

Servings   6

The Home Kitchen Ice Cream Cookbook

Equipment

Cooking pan

Ice cream maker optional

Ice cream container

INGREDIENTS

- 6 egg yolks
- 1/2 cup sugar
- 4 tbsps. date syrup
- 1/4 tsp salt
- 1/2 cup cocoa powder, unsweetened
- 2 cups heavy cream
- 1 cup whole milk
- 1 tsp vanilla extract
- 1 oz. chopped pistachio

DIRECTIONS

1. Add yolks, sugar, date syrup, salt, and cocoa powder in heavy bottom cooking pan.
2. Heat over medium heat and stir constantly until all ingredients are well incorporated. Cook and stir for 5-10 minutes until the mixture thickens and there are no lumps.
3. Let the mixture simmer on low heat but do not boil

Wilson K. Lee

4. Once the custard is thick enough to coat on the spoon, remove from heat.
5. Strain custard with strainer and add vanilla extract and chopped pistachios.
6. Cover and chill at room temperature.
7. If you are making ice cream without ice cream machine, freeze ice cream container for 24 hours beforehand.
8. Pour mixture in container and chill at least 6 hours or overnight to set.
9. Alternatively, churn mixture in an ice cream machine according to manufacturers' instructions.
10. Serve and enjoy!

NUTRITIONAL INFORMATION

Calories Per Servings, 320 kcal, 23.67 g Fat, 24.41 g Total Carbs, 3 g Fibre, 7.1 g Protein

The Home Kitchen Ice Cream Cookbook

Strawberry Custard Ice Cream

Strawberry ice cream is the perfect balance between sour and sweet, especially with fresh homemade puree. You're sure to taste the difference, especially when made with love. WARNING: You may never want store bought again!

Prep Time   10Min

Cooking Time 25 Min

Total Time   35 Min

Servings   6

Wilson K. Lee

Equipment

Cooking pan

Ice cream maker optional

Electric Beater

INGREDIENTS

- ¾ cup whipping cream
- 14 oz. condensed milk
- 4 large egg yolks
- 1 teaspoon vanilla extract
- ¼ teaspoon salt
- 16 oz. fresh strawberries
- 2 tbsp sugar

DIRECTIONS

1. Beat egg yolks in small pan with electric beater.
2. Add whipping cream, and sweetened condensed milk in small pan and simmer for 5 minutes on low heat.
3. Slowly add egg yolk in milk mixture and mix well.
4. Add vanilla extract and salt mixture and stir.
5. Simmer mixture on low heat and stir occasionally, until mixture reaches 160 degrees.

The Home Kitchen Ice Cream Cookbook

6. Once mixture is thick enough to coat on spatula, remove from heat and let it cool to room temperature.
7. While milk mixture is cooling, blend strawberries with sugar in high speed blender.
8. Add strawberries puree in milk mixture and mix well.
9. If you are making ice cream without ice cream machine, freeze ice cream container for 24 hours beforehand.
10. Pour mixture in container and chill at least 6 hours or overnight to set.
11. Alternatively, churn mixture in an ice cream machine according to manufacturers' instructions.
12. Serve ice cream with strawberry slice and enjoy!

NUTRITIONAL INFORMATION

Calories Per Servings, 337 kcal, 14.54 g Fat, 45.37 g Total Carbs, 1.5 g Fibre, 7.84 g Protein

Wilson K. Lee

Lemon Pie Custard Ice Cream

Perfect for summer time, this Lemon Pie Frozen Custard Recipe will be a hit at every cookout. So tart and refreshing; all your friends will be shocked you made it yourself!

Prep Time   10 Min

Cooking Time 25 Min

Total Time   35 Min

Servings   4

Equipment

Cooking pan

The Home Kitchen Ice Cream Cookbook

Ice cream maker optional

Electric Beater

INGREDIENTS

- 3 large eggs yolks
- 1/2 cup sugar
- 1 teaspoon vanilla extract
- Pinch Salt
- 1 cup heavy cream
- 1 cup lemon curd
- Lemon peel slice for topping

DIRECTIONS

1. Beat egg yolks, sugar, vanilla, and salt in small mixing bowl with beater until mixture is creamy.
2. Pour cream into the double boiler over medium heat so that cream dose not boil.
3. Stir cream with wooden spoon to avoid sticking at the bottom.
4. Remove cream from double boiler and slowly add egg mixture in cream and mix well so that there is no lump.
5. Stir constantly until mixture is smooth.
6. Whisking constantly until smooth.

Wilson K. Lee

7. Return mixture to the double boiler and cook for 10-15 over medium-low until mixture is thick

8. Strain the custard with strainer.

9. If you are making ice cream without ice cream machine, freeze ice cream container for 24 hours beforehand.

10. Pour mixture in container and chill at least 6 hours or overnight to set.

11. Alternatively, churn mixture in an ice cream machine according to manufacturers' instructions.

12. Serve ice cream with lemon peel and enjoy!

NUTRITIONAL INFORMATION

Calories Per Servings, 234 kcal, 16.48 g Fat, 16.75 g Total Carbs, 7.6 g Fiber, 4.76 g Protein

The Home Kitchen Ice Cream Cookbook

Blueberry Custard Ice Cream

Blueberries are a well-known antioxidant superfood! What better way to benefit from all the vitamins & minerals than with this creamy treat. Homemade means keeping all the good stuff, and none of the bad.

Prep Time   10 Min

Cooking Time 25 Min

Total Time   35 Min

Servings   4

Wilson K. Lee

Equipment

High Speed Blender

Ice cream maker optional

Electric Beater

INGREDIENTS

CUSTARD BASE

- 1 cup milk
- 1 cup heavy whipped cream
- 4 large eggs
- 4 tbsps. sugar

BLUEBERRY PUREE

- 1 cup fresh blueberries
- 4 tbsps. sugar

BLUEBERRY CHUNKS

- 1/2 cup fresh blueberries

DIRECTIONS

1. Blend all custard ingredients in a high-speed power blender for 2-3 minutes.
2. The speed of the blender will cook the custard because its blades generate energy quickly and eliminates lumps

The Home Kitchen Ice Cream Cookbook

3. Once the custard is blender and cooked in blender, pour it into a bowl.
4. Pour blueberry puree ingredients in blender and blend until smooth.
5. Mix puree with the custard base until incorporated.
6. You can blend puree and custard again in blender for 1 minute if necessary.
7. Chop blueberries in small bowl in small chunks.
8. If you are making ice cream without ice cream machine, freeze ice cream container for 24 hours beforehand.
9. Add chunks into custard and mix well.
10. Pour mixture into container and chill at least 6 hours or overnight to set.
11. Alternatively,, churn mixture in an ice cream machine according to manufacturers' instructions.
12. Serve ice cream with fresh blueberries on top and enjoy!

NUTRITIONAL INFORMATION

Calories Per Servings, 280 kcal, 17.92 g Fat, 25,54 g Total Carbs, 1.5 g Fibre, 5.86 g Protein

Wilson K. Lee

Frozen Banana Custard with Waffles

Move over banana split – there's a new treat in town. Perfect for birthday parties or just a festive night at home, your kids will love to decorate their dessert. BONUS: Fresh bananas = lots of healthy potassium for the monkey in all of us.

Prep Time   10 Min

Cooking Time 25 Min

Total Time   35 Min

Servings   6

Equipment

The Home Kitchen Ice Cream Cookbook

High Speed Blender

Ice cream maker optional

Electric Beater

Cooking pan

Mixing bowl

INGREDIENTS

- 2 cups whole milk
- 3 tbsp liquid glucose
- 10 large egg yolks
- 1/2 cup golden caster sugar
- 1 cup cream cheese
- 3 ripe bananas, blended
- 2 tbsp chocolate spread
- Waffles for serving

DIRECTIONS

1. Simmer milk, liquid glucose in small pan over medium heat.
2. Remove milk mixture from the heat and let it cool at room temperature.

3. Meanwhile, beat eggs and sugar with electric beater in large mixing bowl until mixture become smooth and fluffy.

4. Mix milk mixture, cream cheese, egg mixture in same pan until there is no lump.

5. Return the pan to heat, cook and stir for 5-10 minutes on a low heat.

6. Once the mixture is thick, remove from heat and let it cool.

7. Add banana and mix well, you can blend again in blender.

8. If you are making ice cream without ice cream machine, freeze ice cream container for 24 hours beforehand.

9. Pour mixture in container and chill at least 6 hours or overnight to set.

10. Alternatively, churn mixture in an ice cream machine according to manufacturers' instructions.

11. Drizzle chocolate spread over ice cream scoop.

12. Serve in cups with waffles and enjoy!

NUTRITIONAL INFORMATION

Calories Per Servings, 382 kcal, 24.83 g Fat, 32.15 g Total Carbs, 1.2 g Fibre, 10.27 g Protein

Coffee Custard Chocolate Ice Cream

Bitter coffee cream perfectly balances sweet chocolate chips, for the caffeine fiend in your life. Super quick and easy to make, we won't tell anyone if you opt for this treat instead of your morning cup of joe.

Prep Time   10 Min

Cooking Time 25 Min

Total Time   35 Min

Servings   6

Equipment

Wilson K. Lee

Ice cream maker optional

Electric Beater

Cooking pan

Mixing bowl

INGREDIENTS

- 1 1/2 cups whole milk
- 3/4 cup sugar
- 1 1/2 cups whole coffee beans
- Pinch of salt
- 1 1/2 cups heavy cream
- 5 large egg yolks
- 1/4 teaspoon vanilla extract
- 1/4 teaspoon finely ground coffee
- ½ cup chocolate chips

DIRECTIONS

1. Add milk, sugar, coffee beans, salt, and cream in heavy bottomed pan.
2. Heat them over medium heat until mixture is heated but does not boiled.
3. Once the mixture is heated, remove from heat and let it stand for 1 hour on room temperature.

The Home Kitchen Ice Cream Cookbook

4. Beat eggs in small bowl and slowly pour eggs in milk and stir constable to mix well. Heat and cook for 10 minutes egg and milk mixture again over medium heat until custard thickens.

5. Add cream and stir the custard mixture constantly over medium until the mixture thickens and coats over spoon.

6. Strain mixture through strainer in small bowl.

7. If you are making ice cream without ice cream machine, freeze ice cream container for 24 hours beforehand.

8. Pour mixture in container and chill at least 6 hours or overnight to set.

9. Alternatively, churn mixture in an ice cream machine according to manufacturers' instructions.

10. Serve and enjoy!

NUTRITIONAL INFORMATION

Calories Per Servings, 259 kcal, 17.02 g Fat, 22.48 g Total Carbs, 0 g Fibre, 4.73 g Protein

Wilson K. Lee

Mango Chia Seed Custard Ice Cream

Ready for something new? Stand out from the crowd with this unique summer treat! Fresh tropical mango marries perfectly with superfood chia seeds for a refreshing, nutrient filled favorite!

Prep Time   10 Min

Cooking Time 25 Min

Total Time   35 Min

Servings   8

The Home Kitchen Ice Cream Cookbook

Equipment

Ice cream maker optional

Electric Beater

Cooking pan

Mixing bowl

INGREDIENTS

- 2 cups mango puree
- 1 1/2 cup whole milk
- 2 cups heavy whipped cream
- 5 large egg yolks
- ¾ cup sugar
- 2 tbsps. chia seeds

DIRECTIONS

1. Add the milk, cream and sugar over medium to low heat and cook until all ingredients are mixed and sugar is dissolved.
2. Beat egg yolks in small bowl with electric beater until smooth and creamy.
3. Slowly add egg yolks in milk and cream mixture and stir constantly until smooth.

Wilson K. Lee

4. Return the pan back to heat and cook over low heat stirring constantly.
5. Cook on low heat for 5-10 minutes until the mixture thickens and coats to the spoon.
6. Remove from the heat and let it cool on room temperature.
7. Once custard is chilled add mango puree and chia seeds and mix well.
8. Transfer the ice cream to an ice cream container and freeze for at least 4 hours.
9. Or pour custard in ice cream molds and freeze for overnight.
10. Serve and enjoy.

NUTRITIONAL INFORMATION

Calories Per Servings, 240 kcal, 15.48 g Fat, 22.66 g Total Carbs, 0.7 g Fibre, 4 g Protein

The Home Kitchen Ice Cream Cookbook

Avocado Pistachio Custard Ice Cream

Looking for a creamy treat with low carbs? This rich, no churn Pistachio & Avocado Ice Cream is not only simple to make but a delicious healthy summer treat!

Prep Time   10 Min

Cooking Time 25 Min

Total Time   35 Min

Servings   6

Equipment

Ice cream maker optional

Wilson K. Lee

Electric Beater

Cooking pan

Mixing bowl

Blender

INGREDIENTS

- 1½ cups whole milk
- 1½ cups heavy cream
- 1 cup sugar
- 1 pinch of salt
- 4 egg yolks
- 3 ripe avocados, pitted and peeled
- ½ lemon, juiced
- 1 tsp vanilla
- 1 oz. pistachio, chopped

DIRECTIONS

1. Heat milk, cream, sugar and salt into a sauce pot over medium heat.
2. Once mixture is heat up and starts to boil, remove from heat.
3. Beat egg yolks in another bowl with electric beater until smooth and fluffy.

The Home Kitchen Ice Cream Cookbook

4. Slowly add the milk mixture into the yolks, and stir continuously.
5. Add egg and milk mixture back cooking pan and cook the mixture to 185 degrees or until mixture is thickens to coat on the spoon.
6. Blend avocado and lemon juice into a blender along custard mixture and blend until all ingredients well incorporated.
7. Strain the mixture with a strainer.
8. If you are making ice cream without ice cream machine, freeze ice cream container for 24 hours beforehand.
9. Transfer the ice cream to a freezer-safe container and freeze for at least 4 hours.
10. Or pour custard in ice cream molds and freeze for overnight.
11. Serve a scoop of ice cream with pistachio and mint leaves.
12. Enjoy!

NUTRITIONAL INFORMATION

Calories Per Servings, 450 kcal, 32.87 g Fat, 35.99 g Total Carbs, 7.2 g Fiber, 7.21 g Protein

Wilson K. Lee

Toasted Black Sesame Ice Cream

This toasted black sesame ice cream is sweet and a little nutty, just like your favorite Aunt! A great unique flavor that pairs perfectly with fresh fruit, this is a treat to be rembered.

Prep Time   10 Min

Cooking Time 25 Min

Total Time   35 Min

Servings   8

Equipment

Ice cream maker optional

The Home Kitchen Ice Cream Cookbook

Electric Beater

Cooking pan

Mixing bowl

INGREDIENTS

- 6 oz. light brown sugar
- 4 1/2 oz. egg yolk
- 1/2 teaspoon kosher salt
- 7 oz. heavy cream
- 8 oz. whole milk
- 6 oz. black sesame paste
- 1 tsp. sesame seeds for topping

DIRECTIONS

1. Mix brown sugar, egg yolks, and salt in a pan.
2. Add in cream and milk and cook over low medium heat.
3. Simmer and stir constantly for 5 minutes to avoid and limps on 155°F (68°C).
4. Remove from heat and add black sesame seeds paste.
5. Off heat, whisk in black sesame paste.
6. Strain the mixture with strainer.

Wilson K. Lee

7. If you are making ice cream without ice cream machine, freeze ice cream container for 24 hours beforehand.

8. Pour mixture in ice cream container and freeze overnight to set and harden.

9. Scoop out ice cream in cup, top with toasted sesame seeds.

10. Alternatively, pour machine in ice cream machine to churn according to the manufacturer's directions.

11. Serve and enjoy!

NUTRITIONAL INFORMATION

Calories Per Servings, 325 kcal, 17.93 g Fat, 14.54 g Total Carbs, 1.2 g Fibre, 8.62 g Protein

The Home Kitchen Ice Cream Cookbook

Chapter 2 - Frozen Yogurt Recipes

Coconut Strawberry Frozen Yogurt

For the health conscious this tropical frozen yogurt is perfect for enjoying with your beach bod. If you don't have an ice cream machine, just place the mixture in the freezer and blend by hand every 30 minutes until it reaches desired consistency.

Prep Time   15 Min

Servings   2

Equipment

Wilson K. Lee

High Speed Blender

Mixing bowl

INGREDIENTS

- 2 cups frozen strawberries
- 2 tbsps. agave nectar
- ¼ cup plain yogurt
- 1/2 tbsp. fresh lemon juice
- 1 oz coconut flour
- 1 oz. fresh berries for topping

DIRECTIONS

1. Add the frozen strawberries, agave nectar, yogurt, coconut flour and lemon juice into a food processor and blend for 2-3 minutes.
2. Blend until all ingredients are mixed together and creamy.
3. Make sure there in no lump and mixture is fluffy.
4. If you are making ice cream without ice cream machine, freeze ice cream container for 24 hours beforehand.
5. Pour mixture in airtight container and freeze for about 4 hours or overnight to let it harden
6. Scoop out yogurt in serving bowl.

The Home Kitchen Ice Cream Cookbook

7. Top with fresh berries.
8. Enjoy!

NUTRITIONAL INFORMATION

Calories Per Servings, 131 kcal, 3.14 g Fat, 25.75 g Total Carbs, 4.8 g Fibre, 2.56 g Protein

Wilson K. Lee

Chunky Blackberry Frozen Yogurt

Forgot about that fruit "for smoothies" in the back of your freezer? Lucky for you, this frozen yogurt recipe doesn't mind: combining fresh OR frozen blackberries, yogurt, lemon zest, cardamon, and cinnamon for the perfect balance of flavors.

Prep Time   15 Min

Servings   4

Equipment

High Speed Blender

The Home Kitchen Ice Cream Cookbook

Mixing bowl

INGREDIENTS

- 1½ cup vanilla yogurt
- 1 tbsps. maple syrup
- 2 cups frozen blueberries
- 3 cups blackberries, frozen
- 1 cup blackberries for chunks

DIRECTIONS

1. Add all recipes ingredients in high speed blender and blend for 2-3 minutes on high speed.
2. Add sweetener according to taste, add more if required.
3. Chop blackberries in small bowl in small pieces.
4. Carefully fold chunks in yogurt.
5. If you are making ice cream without ice cream machine, freeze ice cream container for 24 hours beforehand.
6. Pour mixture in ice cream container and place and freeze for 4 hours.
7. Pour scoop of frozen yogurt in serving bowl.
8. Enjoy!

NUTRITIONAL INFORMATION

Calories Per Servings, 180 kcal, 2.35 g Fat, 35.95 g Total Carbs, 9.7 g Fibre, 6.86 g Protein

Wilson K. Lee

Coconut Vanilla Frozen Yogurt

This coconut vanilla frozen yogurt is a great, light twist on a classic summer treat. Add in your favorite frozen fruit for an easy variation!

Prep Time   15 Min

Servings   6

Equipment

High Speed Blender

Mixing bowl

The Home Kitchen Ice Cream Cookbook

INGREDIENTS

- 3 cups nonfat Greek yogurt
- ⅔ cup coconut sugar
- 1 teaspoon vanilla extract
- 2 oz. coconut powder
- 2-3 strawberries
- Fresh strawberries for serving
- Chocolate syrup

DIRECTIONS

1. Blend yogurt, sugar, vanilla, coconut powder and 2-3 strawberries in blender and blend for 2-3 minutes until all ingredients are well incorporated.
2. If you are making ice cream without ice cream machine, freeze ice cream container for 24 hours beforehand.
3. Pour the mixture into ice cream container and freeze for 4 hours until mixture is set.
4. Pour scoop of yogurt in serving plate.
5. Drizzle chocolate syrup over ice cream and serve with strawberries slice.
6. Enjoy!

NUTRITIONAL INFORMATION

Wilson K. Lee

Calories Per Servings, 148 kcal, 3.63 g Fat, 17.29 g Total Carbs, 1 g Fibre, 11.92 g Protein

Hazelnut Chocolate Frozen Yogurt

A creamy frozen chocolate treat you can whip up in seconds, made with items you may already have in your kitchen pantry... and no ice cream machine or blender is required!

Prep Time   15Min

Servings   4

Equipment

High Speed Blender

Mixing bowl

Wilson K. Lee

INGREDIENTS

- 1 cup plain yogurt
- 1/3 cup Chocolate hazelnut spread
- 1 banana
- 1 tsp. vanilla extract
- 2 tbsps. unsweetened cocoa powder
- 2 tbsps. maple syrup
- ½ cup milk
- ¼ cup chocolate syrup for topping

DIRECTIONS

1. Blend all ingredients except chocolate syrup into a high-speed blender.
2. Blend until mixture is smooth and creamy.
3. If you are making ice cream without ice cream machine, freeze ice cream container for 24 hours beforehand.
4. Pour the mixture into a container and freeze for 4 hours until set.
5. Pour scoops of yogurt in serving bowl.
6. Drizzle chocolate syrup on top and enjoy!

NUTRITIONAL INFORMATION

The Home Kitchen Ice Cream Cookbook

Calories Per Servings, 271 kcal, 14.41 g Fat, 26.51 g Total Carbs, 1.5 g Fibre, 7.71 g Protein

Wilson K. Lee

Leche Frozen Coconut Yogurt

Rich Dulce de Leche perfectly balances light coconut yogurt to produce a unique and delicious flavor combo! Quick prep time a no ice cream machine needed make this an easy one to whip up on short notice.

Prep Time   15 Min

Servings   4

Equipment

High Speed Blender

Mixing bowl

The Home Kitchen Ice Cream Cookbook

INGREDIENTS

- 1 1/2 cups coconut yogurt
- 1 cup dulce de leche
- 1 cup heavy cream
- 1/8 teaspoon kosher salt
- 1/2 teaspoon pure vanilla extract (optional)

DIRECTIONS

1. Add all ingredients into a high-speed blender.
2. Blend until mixture is smooth and creamy.
3. If you are making ice cream without ice cream machine, freeze ice cream container for 24 hours beforehand.
4. Pour the mixture into a container and freeze for 4 hours until set.
5. Pour scoops of frozen yogurt in serving bowl.
6. Serve and enjoy!

NUTRITIONAL INFORMATION

Calories Per Servings, 501 kcal, 29.2 g Fat, 59.97 g Total Carbs, 0.2 g Fibre, 1.91 g Protein

Wilson K. Lee

Minty Blueberry Frozen Yogurt

Fresh fruit LOVES mint —my mojito recipe proves it. But this tangy & sweet blueberry frozen yogurt is great summer treat that you can serve for a refreshing breakfast or palette cleansing dessert.

Prep Time   15 Min

Servings   4

Equipment

High Speed Blender

Mixing bowl

The Home Kitchen Ice Cream Cookbook

INGREDIENTS

- 3 cups blueberries, frozen
- 1 cup strawberries
- 2/3 full fat plain Greek yogurt
- 1 tsp freshly cup squeezed lemon juice
- 1 tbsp raw honey
- 1 oz. mint leaves
- I oz. blueberries for topping
- 1 oz. strawberries for topping

DIRECTIONS

1. Add all ingredients into a high-speed blender.
2. Blend until mixture is smooth and creamy.
3. If you are making ice cream without ice cream machine, freeze ice cream container for 24 hours beforehand.
4. Pour the mixture into a container and freeze for 4 hours until set.
5. Pour scoops of frozen yogurt in serving bowl.
6. Serve and enjoy!

NUTRITIONAL INFORMATION

Calories Per Servings, 264 kcal, 1.18 g Fat, 62.5 g Total Carbs, 4.3 g Fibre. 6.78 g Protein

Wilson K. Lee

Chocolate Raspberry Frozen Yogurt

It's quick and easy to prepare, but plan ahead if you're using fresh berries —they take a little longer to freeze. This dessert gives you the best bits in every bite! Any kind of chocolate chip or chunk works great.

Prep Time   15 Min

Servings   2

Equipment

High Speed Blender

Mixing bowl

Wilson K. Lee

INGREDIENTS

- 3 cups raspberries, frozen
- 2/3 cup full fat plain Greek yogurt
- 2 tbsps. maple syrup
- ¼ cup cocoa powder
- Fresh berries for topping

DIRECTIONS

1. Add the frozen raspberries to the blender and blend for 2-3 minutes until smooth and fluffy.
2. Add Greek yogurt and blend with raspberries.
3. Add cocoa powder and honey and blend. Taste and adjust sweetener according to taste.
4. You can use maple syrup instead of honey.
5. If you are making ice cream without ice cream machine, freeze ice cream container for 24 hours beforehand.
6. You can freeze in container for 4 hours until ready.
7. Pour scoops of frozen yogurt in serving bowl.
8. Serve with fresh berries on top.
9. Enjoy!

NUTRITIONAL INFORMATION

Calories Per Servings, 171 kcal, 3.88 g Fat, 34.08 g Total Carbs, 15.2 Fibre, 8.43 g Protein

The Home Kitchen Ice Cream Cookbook

Instant Chocolate Chip Frozen Yogurt

We decided to do something different and turned our whipped recipe into a frozen yogurt! Can we just say- it's amazing! If you are a chocolate lover then you will LOVE this frozen treat this summer. The whipped fluffy texture of the ice cream makes this a perfect, easy, no churn frozen yogurt.

Prep Time   15 Min

Servings   2

Equipment

High Speed Blender

Wilson K. Lee

Mixing bowl

INGREDIENTS

- 2 large ripe bananas, sliced and frozen
- 2 oz. chocolate chips
- 3/4 cup full fat plain Greek yogurt
- 2 tsp pure maple syrup
- Melted chocolate for topping

DIRECTIONS

1. Add the ripe banana to the blender and blend for 2-3 minutes until smooth and fluffy.
2. Add Greek yogurt, maple syrup and chocolate chips and blend with raspberries.
3. Taste and adjust sweetener according to taste.
4. You can use maple syrup instead of honey.
5. This raspberry frozen yogurt is ready to serve.
6. If you are making ice cream without ice cream machine, freeze ice cream container for 24 hours beforehand.
7. You can freeze in container for 4 hours until ready.
8. Pour scoops of frozen yogurt in serving bowl.
9. Serve with melted chocolate on top.
10. Enjoy!

The Home Kitchen Ice Cream Cookbook

NUTRITIONAL INFORMATION

Calories Per Servings, 401 kcal, 13.45 g Fat, 61.71 g Total Carbs, 6.8 g Fibre, 13.64 g Protein

Wilson K. Lee

Peanut Butter Frozen Yogurt

An easy, 6 ingredient recipe for peanut butter frozen yogurt with chocolate chips and nuts throughout! This is a healthier frozen dessert with an amazing tangy, creamy flavour that you will love.

Prep Time   15 Min

Servings   4

Equipment

High Speed Blender

Mixing bowl

The Home Kitchen Ice Cream Cookbook

INGREDIENTS

- 2 large ripe bananas, sliced and frozen
- 1/2 cup full fat plain Greek yogurt
- 1/2 cup creamy natural peanut butter
- Raw honey, as needed
- 1 banana sliced for topping
- 2 tbsps. peanuts for topping
- 2 tbsps. chocolate chips for topping

DIRECTIONS

1. Add the ripe banana to the blender and blend for 2-3 minutes until smooth and fluffy.
2. Add Greek yogurt, maple syrup and chocolate chips and blend with raspberries.
3. Taste and adjust sweetener according to taste.
4. You can use maple syrup instead of honey.
5. This raspberry frozen yogurt is ready to serve.
6. If you are making ice cream without ice cream machine, freeze ice cream container for 24 hours beforehand.
7. You can freeze in container for 4 hours until ready.
8. Pour scoops of frozen yogurt in serving bowl.
9. Serve with melted chocolate on top.
10. Enjoy!

Wilson K. Lee

NUTRITIONAL INFORMATION

Calories Per Servings, 362 kcal, 21.55 g Fat, 35.98 g Total Carbs, 5.6 g Fibre, 12.88 g Protein

Almond Hash Frozen Yogurt

Heavenly Almond Hash Frozen Yogurt is a healthier option than traditional ice cream treats but with all the same delicious flavours you love!

Prep Time   15 Min

Servings   8

Equipment

High Speed Blender

Mixing bowl

Wilson K. Lee

INGREDIENTS

- 2/3 cup brown sugar, packed
- 1/4 cup cocoa powder
- 1 cups strawberry, puree
- 16 oz half and half
- 32 oz Greek Yogurt
- 1 tsp chocolate extract
- 1/4 cup sliced almonds
- 1 oz chocolate chopped,
- 3.5 oz marshmallow cream
- Fresh strawberries in serving

DIRECTIONS

1. Mix brown sugar and cocoa, yogurt and chocolate extract in large mixing bowl.
2. Add in the sliced almonds and chopped chocolate.
3. If you are making ice cream without ice cream machine, freeze ice cream container for 24 hours beforehand.
4. Pour the frozen yogurt mixture into ice cream container and freeze for 1 hour.
5. Add strawberries and swirl marshmallow cream into the mixture, freeze again for 2-3 hours until firm.
6. Serve and enjoy!

The Home Kitchen Ice Cream Cookbook

NUTRITIONAL INFORMATION

Calories Per Servings, 235 kcal, 1.75 g Fat, 42.95 g Total Carbs, 1.3 g Fibre, 13.87 g Protein

Wilson K. Lee

Frozen Yogurt with Black Sesame

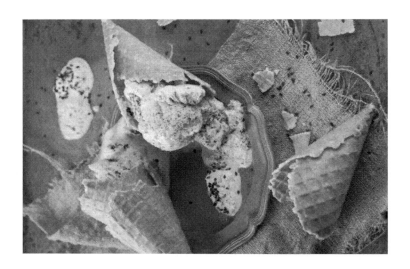

A deliciously different black sesame frozen yoghurt that is sugar free. Black Sesame Ice Cream will be right up your alley if you love peanut butter ice cream. Layered with a ripple of exotic black sesame paste for an entirely new ice cream flavor.

Prep Time   15 Min

Servings   4

Equipment

High Speed Blender

Mixing bowl

The Home Kitchen Ice Cream Cookbook

INGREDIENTS

- 3 tbsps. black sesame seeds
- 2 cups Greek yoghurt
- 2 tsps. Maple syrup

DIRECTIONS

1. Heat heavy bottomed griddle over medium heat, toast the sesame seeds for about 1-2 minutes.
2. Grind seeds in grinder until become smooth paste.
3. Mix the sesame paste with Greek yogurt and other ingredients in mixing bowl.
4. If you are making ice cream without ice cream machine, freeze ice cream container for 24 hours beforehand.
5. Pour mixture in ice cream maker and follow your machines according to manufacturer instructions.
6. Alternatively, pour mixture in ice cream container and freeze for about 4 hours until set.
7. Pour scoops of ice cream in serving bowl.
8. Drizzle sesame seeds on top.
9. Serve and enjoy!

NUTRITIONAL INFORMATION

Calories Per Servings, 105 kcal, 4.11 g Fat, 4.79 g Total Carbs, 0.7 g Fibre, 12.78 g Protein

Wilson K. Lee

Matcha & Coconut Frozen Yogurt

Creamy green tea frozen yogurt with a coconut flour base and avocado. Creamy, healthy and so delicious.

Prep Time   15 Min

Servings   4

Equipment

High Speed Blender

Mixing bowl

The Home Kitchen Ice Cream Cookbook

INGREDIENTS

- 1/2 cup coconut flour
- 1/4 tsp salt
- 2 cups yogurt
- ¼ cup matcha green tea powder
- 1 avocado

DIRECTIONS

1. Add coconut flour, salt, yogurt, matcha powder and avocado in blender and blend until all ingredients are well incorporated.
2. If you are making ice cream without ice cream machine, freeze ice cream container for 24 hours beforehand.
3. Pour mixture in sealable container and freeze in freezer for about 4 hours.
4. Serve and enjoy!

NUTRITIONAL INFORMATION

Calories Per Servings, 191 kcal, 14.7 g Fat, 11.52 g Total Carbs, 4.3 g Fibre, 5.62 g Protein,

Wilson K. Lee

Maple Tahini Frozen Yogurt

Insanely creamy and naturally sweetened yogurt infused with tahini paste and sesame seeds! A healthy and delicious way to indulge in a plant-based dessert or snack.

Prep Time   15 Min

Servings   4

Equipment

High Speed Blender

Mixing bowl

The Home Kitchen Ice Cream Cookbook

INGREDIENTS

- 2 cups full-fat Greek yogurt
- 8 tbsp. maple syrup
- ¼ cup tahini
- 2 tbsps. sesame seeds
- 2 tbsp. lemon juice
- Fresh berries for topping
- Maple syrup for topping

DIRECTIONS

1. Blend, yogurt, maple syrup, tahini and sesame seeds in blender until well incorporated.
2. If you are making ice cream without ice cream machine, freeze ice cream container for 24 hours beforehand.
3. Pour mixture in ice cream container and freeze for about 4 hours until set.
4. Once yogurt is set remove from freezer.
5. Pour scoops of yogurt in serving bowl.
6. Top with fresh berries and maple syrup.
7. Enjoy!

NUTRITIONAL INFORMATION

Calories Per Servings, 195 kcal, 8 g Fat, 30 g Total Carbs, 1.8 g Fibre, 2 g Protein

Wilson K. Lee

2 Berries Frozen Yogurt

A creamy & delicious frozen homemade dessert, made with fresh berries, yogurt and cream. So good you won't even miss regular ice cream!

Prep Time   15 Min

Servings   8

Equipment

High Speed Blender

Mixing bowl

The Home Kitchen Ice Cream Cookbook

INGREDIENTS

- 5 cups frozen blackberries
- 2 cups frozen blueberries
- 2 tablespoons lemon juice
- 1 cup sugar
- 2 teaspoons vanilla extract
- 4 cups fat-free frozen vanilla yogurt

DIRECTIONS

1. Make puree of blackberries and lemon juice in blender.
2. Strain blackberries and discard juice and seeds.
3. Add blackberries pulp again to blender, add sugar and vanilla, blend again for 30 seconds.
4. Mix yogurt, blueberries with blackberry mixture in large mixing bowl. Mix well.
5. If you are making ice cream without ice cream machine, freeze ice cream container for 24 hours beforehand.
6. Pour mixture in ice cream container and freeze for 2-4 until set.
7. Serve scoops of frozen yogurt.
8. Enjoy!

Wilson K. Lee

NUTRITIONAL INFORMATION

Calories Per Servings, 111 kcal, 7 g Fat, 26 g Total Carbs, 7.6 g Fibre, 1 g Protein

Peach Frozen Yogurt with Nuts

This instant peach froyo is made with frozen peaches, Greek yogurt, vanilla and just a touch of honey. You'll love how fast and easy it is to make this quick summertime treat.

Prep Time   15 Min

Servings   4

Equipment

High Speed Blender

Mixing bowl

Wilson K. Lee

INGREDIENTS

- 16 oz. bags frozen peaches
- 3 tbsps. agave nectar
- 1/2 cup plain Greek yogurt
- 1 teaspoon vanilla extract
- 1 oz. chopped nuts
- Peaches slice for topping
- Peach syrup for topping

DIRECTIONS

1. Mix yogurt, honey and vanilla extract in a medium bowl and freeze for 1 hour.
2. Pour frozen yogurt, frozen peaches in blender and blend until all ingredients are mixed and mixture is smooth.
3. Add frozen yogurt to the food processor or blender with the peaches.
4. If you are making ice cream without ice cream machine, freeze ice cream container for 24 hours beforehand.
5. Pour mixture in bowl and freeze again for 2 hours.
6. Once set remove from freezer.
7. Top with peach slice, chopped nuts and peach syrup.
8. Serve and enjoy!

The Home Kitchen Ice Cream Cookbook

NUTRITIONAL INFORMATION

Calories Per Servings, 111 kcal, 26 g Fat, 1 g Total Carbs, 7.6 g Fibre, 1 g Protein

Wilson K. Lee

Mango Frozen Yogurt with Nuts

This Mango Frozen Yogurt takes just minutes to make, has only a few ingredients and requires no ice cream maker. Sweetened only with fruit, what is not to love about this mouthwatering dessert?

Prep Time   15 Min

Servings   4

Equipment

High Speed Blender

Mixing bowl

The Home Kitchen Ice Cream Cookbook

INGREDIENTS

- 4 mangoes, chopped
- 3 tbsps. agave nectar
- 1/2 cup plain Greek yogurt
- 1 teaspoon vanilla extract
- Mango cubes for topping
- Nuts for topping

DIRECTIONS

1. Mix yogurt, honey and vanilla extract in a medium bowl and freeze for 1 hour.
2. Pour frozen mangoes in blender and blend until all ingredients are mixed and mixture is smooth.
3. Add frozen yogurt to the food processor or blender with the mango puree.
4. If you are making ice cream without ice cream machine, freeze ice cream container for 24 hours beforehand.
5. Pour mixture in bowl and freeze again for 2 hours.
6. Once set remove from freezer.
7. Top with mango cubes and nuts.
8. Serve and enjoy!

NUTRITIONAL INFORMATION

Calories Per Servings, 223kcal, 3 g Fat, 51 g Total Carbs, 7.6 g Fibre, 2 g Protein

Wilson K. Lee

Kiwi Frozen Yogurt with Berries

Strawberry-Kiwi has been a long beloved flavor combo for juice boxes, popsicles, or a fresh fruit snack. Now available frozen!

Prep Time   15 Min

Servings   2

Equipment

High Speed Blender

Mixing bowl

The Home Kitchen Ice Cream Cookbook

INGREDIENTS

- 2 cups. Kiwi fruit, chopped
- 3 tbsps. agave nectar
- 1/2 cup plain Greek yogurt
- 1 teaspoon vanilla extract
- Fresh berries for serving

DIRECTIONS

1. Mix yogurt, honey and vanilla extract in a medium bowl and freeze for 1 hour.
2. Pour frozen kiwi fruit in blender and blend until all ingredients are mixed and mixture is smooth.
3. Add frozen yogurt to the food processor or blender with the kiwi fruit.
4. If you are making ice cream without ice cream machine, freeze ice cream container for 24 hours beforehand.
5. Pour mixture in bowl and freeze again for 2 hours.
6. Once set remove from freezer.
7. Top with fresh berries.
8. Serve and enjoy!

NUTRITIONAL INFORMATION

Calories Per Servings, 224 kcal, 2 g Fat, 50 g Total Carbs, 7.6 g Fibre, 3 g Protein

Wilson K. Lee

Cantaloupe Frozen Yogurt

This cantaloupe melon frozen yogurt makes a delicious refreshing summer dessert or snack. Just 5 ingredients for a quick & easy guilt-free treat!

Prep Time   15 Min

Servings   4

Equipment

High Speed Blender

Mixing bowl

The Home Kitchen Ice Cream Cookbook

INGREDIENTS

- 4 cup frozen cantaloupe
- 3 tbsps. agave nectar
- 1/2 cup plain Greek yogurt
- 1 teaspoon vanilla extract
- Cantaloupe slice for topping

DIRECTIONS

1. Mix yogurt, honey and vanilla extract in a medium bowl and freeze for 1 hour.
2. Pour cantaloupe in blender and blend until all ingredients are mixed and mixture is smooth.
3. Add frozen yogurt to the food processor or blender with the cantaloupe
4. If you are making ice cream without ice cream machine, freeze ice cream container for 24 hours beforehand.
5. Pour mixture in bowl and freeze again for 2 hours.
6. Once set remove from freezer.
7. Serve scoop with cantaloupe slice.
8. Enjoy!

NUTRITIONAL INFORMATION

Calories Per Servings, 243 kcal, 7 g Fat, 39 g Total Carbs, 7.6 g Fibre, 2 g Protein

Wilson K. Lee

Avocado Frozen Yogurt

Wow all your health nut friends with this Avocado Frozen Yogurt sweetened with agave nectar and vanilla. Blended together for a uniquely healthy superfood treat!

Prep Time   15 Min

Servings   4

Equipment

High Speed Blender

Mixing bowl

The Home Kitchen Ice Cream Cookbook

INGREDIENTS

- 2 avocado fruit, chopped and frozen
- 3 tbsps. agave nectar
- 1/2 cup plain Greek yogurt
- 1 teaspoon vanilla extract
- Raspberries for topping
- Pistachio for topping

DIRECTIONS

1. Mix yogurt, honey and vanilla extract in a medium bowl and freeze for 1 hour.
2. Pour avocado in blender and blend until mixed and mixture is smooth.
3. Add frozen yogurt to the food processor or blender with the avocado.
4. If you are making ice cream without ice cream machine, freeze ice cream container for 24 hours beforehand.
5. Pour mixture in bowl and freeze again for 2 hours.
6. Once set remove from freezer.
7. Top scoop of yogurt with raspberries and pistachio.
8. Serve and enjoy!

NUTRITIONAL INFORMATION

Calories Per Servings, 183 kcal, 15 g Fat, 10 g Total Carbs, 7.6 g Fibre, 3 g Protein

Wilson K. Lee

Coconut Almond Frozen Yogurt

This frozen yogurt isn't just delicious, it's fun to make! The coconut and almond flavors are rich and taste amazing when drizzled with nuts and blended with cocoa powder.

Prep Time   15 Min

Servings   2

Equipment

High Speed Blender

Mixing bowl

INGREDIENTS

The Home Kitchen Ice Cream Cookbook

- ½ cup coconut flour
- 3 tbsps. agave nectar
- 1/2 cup plain Greek yogurt
- 1 teaspoon vanilla extract
- 1 tbsps. cocoa powder
- 1 oz. chopped almonds

DIRECTIONS

1. Mix yogurt, honey and vanilla extract in a medium bowl and freeze for 1 hour.
2. Pour frozen yogurt, and all ingredients in blender and blend until all ingredients are mixed and mixture is smooth.
3. If you are making ice cream without ice cream machine, freeze ice cream container for 24 hours beforehand.
4. Pour mixture in bowl and freeze again for 2 hours.
5. Once ice cream set remove from freezer.
6. Top scoop of yogurt with chopped almonds.
7. Serve and enjoy!

NUTRITIONAL INFORMATION

Calories Per Servings, 186 kcal, 7 g Fat, 4 g Total Carbs, 7.6 g Fibre, 2 g Protein

Wilson K. Lee

Chocolate Chip Frozen Yogurt

This chocolate chip frozen yogurt is so dreamy creamy and tastes just like cookie dough. So incredibly easy to make, you'll be wondering why you haven't made it sooner!

Prep Time   15 Min

Servings   4

Equipment

High Speed Blender

Mixing bowl

The Home Kitchen Ice Cream Cookbook

INGREDIENTS

- 4 bananas, frozen
- 3 tbsps. agave nectar
- 1/2 cup plain Greek yogurt
- 1 teaspoon vanilla extract
- ¼ cup chocolate chip

DIRECTIONS

1. Mix yogurt, honey and vanilla extract in a medium bowl and freeze for 1 hour.
2. Pour frozen banana in blender and blend until mixed and mixture is smooth.
3. Add frozen yogurt to the food processor or blender with the banana.
4. Carefully fold in chocolate chip.
5. If you are making ice cream without ice cream machine, freeze ice cream container for 24 hours beforehand.
6. Pour mixture in bowl and freeze again for 2 hours.
7. Once set remove from freezer.
8. Top scoop of yogurt banana slice.
9. Serve and enjoy!

NUTRITIONAL INFORMATION

Calories Per Servings, 134 kcal, 2 g Fat, 30 g Total Carbs, 7.6 g Fibre, 1 g Protein

87

Wilson K. Lee

Coconut Cashew Frozen Yogurt

A delicious and very healthy yogurt that is raw, sugar free and gluten-free. It's easy to make too!

Prep Time   15 Min

Servings   4

Equipment

High Speed Blender

Mixing bowl

Ice cream container

The Home Kitchen Ice Cream Cookbook

INGREDIENTS

- 1 cup coconut flour
- ½ cup cashew
- 3 tbsps. agave nectar
- 1 cup plain Greek yogurt
- 1 teaspoon vanilla extract

DIRECTIONS

1. Mix yogurt, honey and vanilla extract in a medium bowl and freeze for 1 hour.
2. Pour coconut and cashew in blender and blend until mixture is smooth.
3. Add frozen yogurt to the food processor or blender with the nuts.
4. If you are making ice cream without ice cream machine, freeze ice cream container for 24 hours beforehand.
5. Pour mixture in bowl and freeze again for 2 hours.
6. Once set remove from freezer.
7. Top scoop of yogurt with coconut flour.
8. Serve and enjoy!

NUTRITIONAL INFORMATION

Wilson K. Lee

Calories Per Servings, 247 kcal, 19 g Fat, 14 g Total Carbs, 7.6 g Fibre, 6 g Protein

The Home Kitchen Ice Cream Cookbook

Chapter 3 - Gelato Recipes

Simple Berry Gelato

Gelato is a classic favorite enjoyed all around the world. This easy to make foolproof recipe will work in your ice cream maker too!

Prep Time   15 Min

Servings   4

Equipment

Wilson K. Lee

High Speed Blender

Mixing bowl

Ice cream container

INGREDIENTS

- 1½ cup vanilla yogurt
- 1 Tablespoon honey, optional
- 2 cups frozen blueberries
- 3 cups strawberries, frozen

DIRECTIONS

1. Add ingredients in the high-speed blender and blend until mixture is creamy.
2. Adjust sweetener according to taste.
3. Blend mixture again until all ingredients are well incorporated.
4. If you are making ice cream without ice cream machine, freeze ice cream container for 24 hours beforehand.
5. Pour mixture in bowl and freeze again for 2 hours.
6. Once set remove from freezer.
7. Top scoop of yogurt with strawberry slice.
8. Serve and enjoy!

NUTRITIONAL INFORMATION

The Home Kitchen Ice Cream Cookbook

Calories Per Servings, 168 kcal, 1 g Fat, 34 g Total Carbs, 7.6 g Fibre, 5 g Protein

Wilson K. Lee

Strawberry Homemade Gelato

To guarantee homemade luscious consistency and purity of flavor, you can thicken gelato with cornstarch rather than eggs. The result has less palate-coating fat than ice cream and lets the fruit shine.

Prep Time   10 Min

Cooking time   20 Min

Total Time   30 Min

Servings   6

The Home Kitchen Ice Cream Cookbook

Equipment

High Speed Blender

Mixing bowl

Ice cream container

INGREDIENTS

- 2 cups whole milk
- 4 large egg yolks, room temperature
- 3/4 cup granulated sugar
- 1 cup heavy whipping cream
- 3/4 teaspoon salt
- 2 teaspoons vanilla extract
- 1 1/4 cups strawberries, pureed
- 1 tablespoon sugar

DIRECTIONS

1. Heat milk in cooking pan over medium heat.
2. Simmer for about 3-4 minutes on low heat.
3. Meanwhile, beat egg yolks with sugar in small bowl until mixture creamy.
4. Remove from heat and set aside
5. Add egg mixture in milk mixture and mix continuously.
6. Return custard pan to heat and cook again.

Wilson K. Lee

7. Cook and stir with wooden spoon for 4-5 minutes on low temperature until mixture is thick and coat on spoon.
8. Cook, stirring frequently with a wooden spoon.
9. Do not bring custard to boil.
10. Strain the mixture with strain and remove and impurity.
11. Add rest of the ingredients with custard in blender and blend until well incorporated.
12. If you are making ice cream without ice cream machine, freeze ice cream container for 24 hours beforehand.
13. Pour the mixture in ice cream container and place in the refrigerator for about 2 hours until the mixture reaches 40 degrees F or below.
14. Alternatively, pour the mixture into an ice cream maker and run maker according to manufacture instructions until required consistency reach.
15. Serve scoop of gelato in bowl with fresh berries.
16. Serve and enjoy!

NUTRITIONAL INFORMATION

Calories Per Servings, 246 kcal, 4 g Fat, 27 g Total Carbs, 7.6 g Fibre, 4 g Protein

Lemon Gelato

Lemon gelato is so refreshing, and this recipe is so incredibly easy to make! It's real gelato, by the actual definition. You don't even need an ice cream maker.

Prep Time   10 Min

Cooking time 30 Min

Total Time   40 Min

Servings   6

Wilson K. Lee

Equipment

High Speed Blender

Mixing bowl

Ice cream container

INGREDIENTS

- 1 cup whole milk
- 1 cup sugar
- 5 large egg yolks, lightly beaten
- 3 tablespoons grated lemon zest
- 3/4 cup fresh lemon juice (about 5 lemons)
- 2 cups heavy whipping cream

DIRECTIONS

1. Heat milk in cooking pan over medium heat.
2. Add sugar in milk and cook for 2-3 minutes until sugar is dissolved.
3. Beat egg yolks in small bowl and slowly add in milk mixture.
4. Stir and simmer on low heat for 4-5 minutes until mixture become thick.
5. Add lemon zest and lemon juice and mix well.

The Home Kitchen Ice Cream Cookbook

6. If you are making ice cream without ice cream machine, freeze ice cream container for 24 hours beforehand.

7. Pour the mixture in ice cream container and place in the refrigerator for about 2 hours until the mixture reaches 40 degrees F or below.

8. Alternatively, pour the mixture into an ice cream maker and run maker according to manufacture instructions until required consistency reach.

9. Serve scoop of gelato in bowl.

10. Serve and enjoy!

NUTRITIONAL INFORMATION

Calories Per Servings, 294 kcal, 19 g Fat, 26 g Total Carbs, 7.6 g Fibre, 4 g Protein

Wilson K. Lee

Stracciatella Gelato

Stracciatella gelato is such a simple recipe that it demands the best of the best; seek out high-quality chocolate and milk for great results.

Prep Time   10Min

Cooking time 15 Min

Total Time   25 Min

Servings   6

Equipment

High Speed Blender

The Home Kitchen Ice Cream Cookbook

Mixing bowl

Ice cream container

Cooking Pan

INGREDIENTS

- 2 cups whole milk
- 3/4 cup sugar
- 1 vanilla bean, split lengthwise
- 4 egg yolks
- 1 cup heavy cream
- 4 ounces bittersweet chocolate, coarsely chopped

DIRECTIONS

1. Heat milk in cooking pan over medium heat.
2. Add sugar in milk and cook for 2-3 minutes until sugar is dissolved.
3. Beat egg yolks in small bowl and slowly add in milk mixture.
4. Stir and simmer on low heat for 4-5 minutes until mixture become thick.
5. Add cream and beans paste and mix well.
6. Carefully fold chocolate in mixture.

7. If you are making ice cream without ice cream machine, freeze ice cream container for 24 hours beforehand.

8. Pour the mixture in ice cream container and place in the refrigerator for about 2 hours until the mixture reaches 40 degrees F or below.

9. Alternatively, pour the mixture into an ice cream maker and run maker according to manufacture instructions until required consistency reach.

10. Serve scoop of gelato in bowl.

11. Serve and enjoy!

NUTRITIONAL INFORMATION

Calories Per Servings, 280 kcal, 13 g Fat, 36 g Total Carbs, 7.6 g Fibre, 5 g Protein

The Home Kitchen Ice Cream Cookbook

Chocolate-Hazelnut Gelato

This decadent hazelnut gelato recipe is made with homemade hazelnut butter and flecked with dark chocolate for the ultimate Nutella treat!

Prep Time   10Min

Cooking time 15 Min

Total Time   25 Min

Servings   6

Equipment

High Speed Blender

Wilson K. Lee

Mixing bowl

Ice cream container

INGREDIENTS

- 2 cups whole milk
- 1 cup heavy cream
- 1/2 cup sugar, plus 1/4 cup
- 4 egg yolks
- 1/2 teaspoon vanilla extract
- 1/2 cup chocolate-hazelnut spread
- 1/2 cup toasted hazelnuts, crushed, for garnish

DIRECTIONS

1. Heat milk in cooking pan over medium heat.
2. Add sugar in milk and cook for 2-3 minutes until sugar is dissolved.
3. Beat egg yolks in small bowl and slowly add in milk mixture.
4. Stir and simmer on low heat for 4-5 minutes until mixture become thick.
5. Add cream, chocolate hazelnuts and toasted hazelnuts in mixture and mix well.

The Home Kitchen Ice Cream Cookbook

6. Pour the mixture in ice cream container and place in the refrigerator for about 2 hours until the mixture reaches 40 degrees F or below.
7. Alternatively, pour the mixture into an ice cream maker and run maker according to manufacture instructions until required consistency reach.
8. Serve scoop of gelato in bowl with hazelnuts on top.
9. Serve and enjoy!

NUTRITIONAL INFORMATION

Calories Per Servings, 283 kcal, 19 g Fat, 21 g Total Carbs, 7.6 g Fibre, 6 g Protein

Wilson K. Lee

Chocolate Gelato

It's important to use good quality ingredients when making gelato because there's a lower fat content. Here is a recipe inspired by my Italian travels: dark chocolate gelato with added chocolate – homemade with love.

Prep Time   10Min

Cooking time 15 Min

Total Time   25 Min

Servings   6

The Home Kitchen Ice Cream Cookbook

Equipment

High Speed Blender

Mixing bowl

Ice cream container

INGREDIENTS

- 4 ounces semisweet or bittersweet chocolate, finely chopped
- 3 cups organic whole milk
- 2 large egg yolks
- 3/4 cup granulated organic cane sugar
- ¼ tsp sea salt
- ½ cup unsweetened cocoa powder
- ½ tsp vanilla extract

DIRECTIONS

1. Heat milk in cooking pan over medium heat.
2. Add sugar in milk and cook for 2-3 minutes until sugar is dissolved.
3. Beat egg yolks in small bowl and slowly add in milk mixture.
4. Stir and simmer on low heat for 4-5 minutes until mixture become thick.

5. Add chocolate, cocoa powder and vanilla in mixture and mix well.
6. If you are making ice cream without ice cream machine, freeze ice cream container for 24 hours beforehand.
7. Pour the mixture in ice cream container and place in the refrigerator for about 2 hours until the mixture reaches 40 degrees F or below.
8. Alternatively, pour the mixture into an ice cream maker and run maker according to manufacture instructions until required consistency reach.
9. Serve scoop of gelato in bowl.
10. Serve and enjoy!

NUTRITIONAL INFORMATION

Calories Per Servings, 260 kcal, 17.93 g Fat, 63.99 g Total Carbs, 7.6 g Fibre, 9.59 g Protein

The Home Kitchen Ice Cream Cookbook

Smores Gelato with Nutella

S'mores Gelato filled with graham crackers, chocolate, and toasted marshmallows. This recipe makes the perfect s'more ice cream to bring back campfire memories!

Prep Time   10Min

Cooking time 15 Min

Total Time   25 Min

Servings   6

Wilson K. Lee

Equipment

High Speed Blender

Mixing bowl

Ice cream container

Cooking pan

INGREDIENTS

- 2 cups milk
- 1 cup granulated sugar
- 3/4 cup cream
- 2 egg yolks
- 1 teaspoon vanilla bean paste
- 1/4 cup Nutella

DIRECTIONS

1. Add milk in cooking pan and cook over medium heat.
2. Beat egg yolk with sugar in another bowl and make creamy mixture.
3. Slowly add egg mixture in milk and mix continuously with wooden spoon.
4. Add cream and vanilla in mixture and mix well.
5. Strain the mixture with strainer and remove any solids

The Home Kitchen Ice Cream Cookbook

6. If you are making ice cream without ice cream machine, freeze ice cream container for 24 hours beforehand.

7. Pour the mixture in ice cream container and place in the refrigerator for about 2 hours until the mixture reaches 40 degrees F or below.

8. Alternatively, pour the mixture into an ice cream maker and run maker according to manufacture instructions until required consistency reach.

9. Serve scoop of gelato in bowl and top with Nutella.

10. Serve and enjoy!

NUTRITIONAL INFORMATION

Calories Per Servings, 259 kcal, 17.93 g Fat, 63.99 g Total Carbs, 7.6 g Fibre, 9.59 g Protein

Wilson K. Lee

Avocado gelato

This avocado gelato is a very easy & healthy homemade ice cream that can be made vegan, paleo-friendly and absolutely tasty. Creamy, smooth and ultra-rich with no ice cream maker.

Prep Time   10 Min

Cooking time 15 Min

Total Time   25 Min

Servings   6

The Home Kitchen Ice Cream Cookbook

Equipment

High Speed Blender

Mixing bowl

Ice cream container

INGREDIENTS

- 1/2 cup whole milk
- 2 tablespoons cornstarch
- 1 1/2 cups fat-free milk
- 1/2 cup sugar
- 4 strips orange zest
- 2 ripe avocados
- 2 tablespoons fresh lime juice, plus wedges for serving
- 1/4 teaspoon coarse salt

DIRECTIONS

1. Mix milk with corn starch in bowl and set aside.
2. Mix fat-free milk, sugar, and orange zest in a saucepan and heat on medium heat.
3. Simmer on low heat and add corn starch mixture slowly.
4. Bring the mixture to boil and stir constantly

Wilson K. Lee

5. Once thick remove from heat and let it cool on room temperature.
6. Blend milk with avocados, lime juice, and salt in a food processor until mixture is creamy.
7. If you are making ice cream without ice cream machine, freeze ice cream container for 24 hours beforehand.
8. Pour the mixture in ice cream container and place in the refrigerator for about 2 hours until the mixture reaches 40 degrees F or below.
9. Alternatively, pour the mixture into an ice cream maker and run maker according to manufacture instructions until required consistency reach.
10. Serve scoop of gelato in bowl with chocolate chip on top.
11. Serve and enjoy!

NUTRITIONAL INFORMATION

Calories Per Servings, 191 kcal, 17.93 g Fat, 63.99 g Total Carbs, 7.6 g Fibre, 9.59 g Protein

Pistachio Gelato

Pistachio gelato is an Italian favorite made with pistachio nuts or flavoring which create its distinctively green color. Try drizzled with chocolate syrup for a more indulgent treat.

Prep Time   10 Min

Cooking time 15 Min

Total Time   25 Min

Servings   6

Equipment

High Speed Blender

Wilson K. Lee

Mixing bowl

Ice cream container

INGREDIENTS

- 2 cups milk
- 1 cup heavy whipping cream
- 4 egg yolks
- 1/2 cup sugar
- 1/3 cup pistachio nut paste
- 1/3 cup shelled and roasted pistachios optional

DIRECTIONS

1. Add milk and heavy whipping cream in a cooking pan and heat over medium-high heat.
2. Simmer on low heat for 2-3 minutes.
3. Meanwhile, beat egg yolks with sugar in bowl with electric beater.
4. Remove milk from heat and add egg mixture in milk. Mix well.
5. Transfer cooking pan to heat and cook for 4-5 minutes, stir continuously to avoid any lump.
6. Add pistachio and mix well.

The Home Kitchen Ice Cream Cookbook

7. If you are making ice cream without ice cream machine, freeze ice cream container for 24 hours beforehand.

8. Pour the mixture in ice cream container and place in the refrigerator for about 2 hours until the mixture reaches 40 degrees F or below.

9. Alternatively, pour the mixture into an ice cream maker and run maker according to manufacture instructions until required consistency reach.

10. Serve scoop of gelato in bowl with pistachio on top.

11. Serve and enjoy!

NUTRITIONAL INFORMATION

Calories Per Servings, 264 kcal, 17.93 g Fat, 63.99 g Total Carbs, 7.6 g Fibre, 9.59 g Protein

Wilson K. Lee

Vanilla Cappuccino Gelato

This stunning vanilla cappuccino gelato recipe is a luxuriously creamy summer treat, with cinnamon, espresso, and vanilla creating the perfect balance of bitter and sweet.

Prep Time   10Min

Cooking time 15 Min

Total Time   25 Min

Servings   6

The Home Kitchen Ice Cream Cookbook

Equipment

High Speed Blender

Mixing bowl

Ice cream container

Cooking pan

INGREDIENTS

- 2 cups whole milk, the best quality you can find
- ½ cup whipping cream
- 2 tbsps. skimmed milk powder
- ¼ cup caster sugar
- 4 tbsps. liquid glucose
- 1 tsp. cinnamon powder
- 1 tsp. vanilla extract
- 1 tsp. espresso

DIRECTIONS

1. Pour milk and cream in cooking pan and cook over medium heat.
2. Mix all dry ingredients in bowl and slowly add in milk, stir continuously.
3. Stir with wooden spoon until all ingredients are well incorporated.

Wilson K. Lee

4. If you are making ice cream without ice cream machine, freeze ice cream container for 24 hours beforehand.

5. Pour the mixture in ice cream container and place in the refrigerator for about 2 hours until the mixture reaches 40 degrees F or below.

6. Alternatively, pour the mixture into an ice cream maker and run maker according to manufacture instructions until required consistency reach.

7. Serve and enjoy!

NUTRITIONAL INFORMATION

Calories Per Servings, 105 kcal, 3 g Fat, 15 g Total Carbs, 7.6 g Fibre, 2 g Protein

The Home Kitchen Ice Cream Cookbook

Yogurt Gelato

The perfect combination of two fan favorites: Frozen Yogurt & Gelato create the optimal creamy texture and light tangy taste, a perfect pairing with any fresh fruit.

Prep Time   10 Min

Cooking time 15 Min

Total Time   25 Min

Servings   6

Equipment

Wilson K. Lee

High Speed Blender

Mixing bowl

Ice cream container

INGREDIENTS

- 2 cups whole milk
- 1 cup heavy whipping cream
- 4 egg yolks
- 3/4 cup sugar, divided
- Pinch kosher salt
- 1 tablespoon hot water
- 1 teaspoon freshly squeezed lemon juice
- 2 cups Greek yogurt

DIRECTIONS

1. Heat milk in cooking pan over medium heat.
2. Add sugar in milk and cook for 2-3 minutes until sugar is dissolved.
3. Beat egg yolks in small bowl and slowly add in milk mixture.
4. Stir and simmer on low heat for 4-5 minutes until mixture become thick.

The Home Kitchen Ice Cream Cookbook

5. Add cream, yogurt, lemon juice in milk mixture and mix well.
6. If you are making ice cream without ice cream machine, freeze ice cream container for 24 hours beforehand.
7. Pour the mixture in ice cream container and place in the refrigerator for about 2 hours until the mixture reaches 40 degrees F or below.
8. Alternatively, pour the mixture into an ice cream maker and run maker according to manufacture instructions until required consistency reach.
9. Serve scoop of gelato in bowl fresh fruits.
10. Serve and enjoy!

NUTRITIONAL INFORMATION

Calories Per Servings, 277 kcal, 17.93 g Fat, 63.99 g Total Carbs, 7.6 g Fibre, 9.59 g Protein

Wilson K. Lee

Creamy Basil Gelato

This creamy Basil Ice Cream takes me straight back to Italy! There's something magical about the combination of cream, basil and this hint of lemon that will make you fall in love with this unusual ice cream flavor!

Prep Time   10Min

Cooking time 15 Min

Total Time   25 Min

Servings   6

The Home Kitchen Ice Cream Cookbook

Equipment

High Speed Blender

Mixing bowl

Ice cream container

Cooking pan

INGREDIENTS

- ½ cup sugar
- 1 lemon juice
- 1 oz. basil leaves
- 2 cups cream
- 1 cup full fat milk
- 1/2 tsp salt
- 5 large egg yolks

DIRECTIONS

1. Heat milk in cooking pan over medium heat.
2. Add sugar in milk and cook for 2-3 minutes until sugar is dissolved.
3. Beat egg yolks in small bowl and slowly add in milk mixture.
4. Stir and simmer on low heat for 4-5 minutes until mixture become thick.

Wilson K. Lee

5. Add cream basil leaves salt and lemon juice mix well and seep for 1 hour.
6. Strain the mixture with strainer.
7. If you are making ice cream without ice cream machine, freeze ice cream container for 24 hours beforehand.
8. Pour the mixture in ice cream container and place in the refrigerator for about 2 hours until the mixture reaches 40 degrees F or below.
9. Alternatively, pour the mixture into an ice cream maker and run maker according to manufacture instructions until required consistency reach.
10. Serve scoop of gelato in bowl with maple syrup on top.
11. Serve and enjoy!

NUTRITIONAL INFORMATION

Calories Per Servings, 257 kcal, 20 g Fat, 14 g Total Carbs, 7.6 g Fibre, 5 g Protein

Cinnamon Gelato

A great holiday season treat, this cinnamon gelato comes together in 15 minutes (plus freezing), without an ice cream machine.

Prep Time   10Min

Cooking time 15 Min

Total Time   25 Min

Servings   6

Equipment

High Speed Blender

Wilson K. Lee

Mixing bowl

Ice cream container

INGREDIENTS

- 2 cups whole milk
- 1 cup heavy cream
- 4 large egg yolks
- 2/3 cup sugar
- 1/4 teaspoon pure vanilla extract
- 2 teaspoons ground cinnamon

DIRECTIONS

1. Heat milk in cooking pan over medium heat.
2. Add sugar in milk and cook for 2-3 minutes until sugar is dissolved.
3. Beat egg yolks in small bowl and slowly add in milk mixture.
4. Stir and simmer on low heat for 4-5 minutes until mixture become thick.
5. Add cream, vanilla and cinnamon powder in mixture and mix well.
6. If you are making ice cream without ice cream machine, freeze ice cream container for 24 hours beforehand.

The Home Kitchen Ice Cream Cookbook

7. Pour the mixture in ice cream container and place in the refrigerator for about 2 hours until the mixture reaches 40 degrees F or below.
8. Alternatively, pour the mixture into an ice cream maker and run maker according to manufacture instructions until required consistency reach.
9. Serve scoop of gelato in bowl with roasted pumpkin seeds on top.
10. Serve and enjoy!

NUTRITIONAL INFORMATION

Calories Per Servings, 225 kcal, 17.93 g Fat, 63.99 g Total Carbs, 7.6 g Fibre, 9.59 g Protein

Wilson K. Lee

Sour Cream Gelato

This fabulous 5-ingredient gelato is easy to make, with the perfect balance of tangy sour cream and sweet blueberries. For the smoothest texture, allow the base mixture to chill in your refrigerator overnight before freezing.

Prep Time   10Min

Cooking time 15 Min

Total Time   25 Min

Servings   6

The Home Kitchen Ice Cream Cookbook

Equipment

High Speed Blender

Mixing bowl

Ice cream container

Cooking pan

INGREDIENTS

- 2 tablespoons cornstarch
- 2 1/4 cups whole milk, divided
- 1 1/3 cups granulated sugar
- 1 1/2 cups sour cream
- 2 cups blueberries

DIRECTIONS

1. Mix cornstarch with some milk in a small bowl and set aside.
2. Add sugar and milk in pan heat over medium heat.
3. Simmer and stir on low heat until sugar is dissolved
4. Remove pan from heat and slowly add cornstarch slurry in milk and mix well.
5. Return pan on heat and cook for about 8-10 minutes, stir continuously.

Wilson K. Lee

6. Once mixture is thick remove from heat and let it cool on room temperature.

7. Once mixture is cool add sour cream and blend in blender.

8. If you are making ice cream without ice cream machine, freeze ice cream container for 24 hours beforehand.

9. Pour the mixture in ice cream container and place in the refrigerator for about 2 hours until the mixture reaches 40 degrees F or below.

10. Alternatively, pour the mixture into an ice cream maker and run maker according to manufacture instructions until required consistency reach.

11. Serve scoop of gelato in bowl.

12. Serve and enjoy!

NUTRITIONAL INFORMATION

Calories Per Servings, 332 kcal, 9 g Fat, 59 g Total Carbs, 7.6 g Fibre, 5 g Protein

Mango Gelato

This simple gelato is perfect for warm summer nights and is a snap to throw together with your ripe summer mangoes!

Prep Time   10Min

Cooking time 15 Min

Total Time   25 Min

Servings   6

Equipment

High Speed Blender

Wilson K. Lee

Mixing bowl

Ice cream container

INGREDIENTS

- 3 yellow mangos, peeled and cubed (about 2 cups)
- ¼ cup granulated sugar
- 1 ½ cups whole milk
- ½ cup heavy whipping cream
- 1 tbsp lemon juice

DIRECTIONS

1. Add mangoes, sugar, and milk, cream and lemon juice in high speed blender and blend all ingredients for 2-3 minutes.
2. Freeze mixture for 1 hour.
3. Pour the mixture again in blender and blend.
4. If you are making ice cream without ice cream machine, freeze ice cream container for 24 hours beforehand.
5. Pour the mixture in ice cream container and place in the refrigerator for about 2 hours until the mixture reaches 40 degrees F or below.

The Home Kitchen Ice Cream Cookbook

6. Alternatively, pour the mixture into an ice cream maker and run maker according to manufacture instructions until required consistency reach.
7. Serve scoop of gelato in bowl with coconut flour on top.
8. Serve and enjoy!

NUTRITIONAL INFORMATION

Calories Per Servings, 106 kcal, 5 g Fat, 12 g Total Carbs, 7.6 g Fibre, 2 g Protein

Wilson K. Lee

Vegan Mango Gelato

Creamy and divinely textured vegan mango gelato. This easy 4-ingredient recipe is perfectly sweet, has a gorgeous color and all the mango flavor you could dream of!

Prep Time   10Min

Cooking time 15 Min

Total Time   25 Min

Servings   6

The Home Kitchen Ice Cream Cookbook

Equipment

High Speed Blender

Mixing bowl

Ice cream container

INGREDIENTS

- 1-1/2cup mango flesh
- 1/3 cup cashew cream
- 2-3 dates
- 1 tsp vanilla extract

DIRECTIONS

1. Place all ingredients in a high-speed blender and blend until all ingredients are well incorporated.
2. If you are making ice cream without ice cream maker then freeze ice cream container for 24 hours.
3. Pour the mixture in ice cream container and place in the refrigerator for about 2 hours until the mixture reaches 40 degrees F or below.
4. Alternatively, pour the mixture into an ice cream maker and run maker according to manufacture instructions until required consistency reach.
5. Serve scoop of gelato in bowl.
6. Serve and enjoy!

Wilson K. Lee

NUTRITIONAL INFORMATION

Calories Per Servings, 205 kcal, 17.93 g Fat, 63.99 g Total Carbs, 7.6 g Fibre, 9.59 g Protein

The Home Kitchen Ice Cream Cookbook

Vegan Coffee Gelato

The vegan coffee gelato is perfect for a healthy and delicious kick of energy at no animals expense. Leave out the vegan chocolate chips for an even healthier alternative!

Prep Time   10 Min

Cooking time 15 Min

Total Time   25 Min

Servings   6

Wilson K. Lee

Equipment

High Speed Blender

Mixing bowl

Ice cream container

INGREDIENTS

- 1-1/2 cup cashew creamer
- 1/2 cup cashews (soaked overnight)
- 5 dates
- 2 tbsp ground coffee
- 1 tsp cacao powder
- 1 Tbsp hazelnut butter
- 1 tsp vanilla extract
- 1/2 tsp cinnamon
- 1/4 tsp nutmeg
- Pinch of salt
- 1 oz vegan chocolate chips

DIRECTIONS

1. Place all ingredients in a high-speed blender and blend until all ingredients are well incorporated.
2. Carefully fold in chocolate chip in mixture.

The Home Kitchen Ice Cream Cookbook

3. If you are making ice cream without ice cream maker then freeze ice cream container for 24 hours.

4. Pour the mixture in ice cream container and place in the refrigerator for about 2 hours until the mixture reaches 40 degrees F or below.

5. Alternatively, pour the mixture into an ice cream maker and run maker according to manufacture instructions until required consistency reach.

6. Serve scoop of gelato in bowl.

7. Serve and enjoy!

NUTRITIONAL INFORMATION

Calories Per Servings, 363 kcal, 17.93 g Fat, 63.99 g Total Carbs, 7.6 g Fibre, 9.59 g Protein

Wilson K. Lee

Vegan Chocolate Gelato

Make the most of your vegan chocolate with this great alternative recipe. Sweet treats always taste better when they're also good for the environment!

Prep Time   10Min

Cooking time 15 Min

Total Time   25 Min

Servings   6

The Home Kitchen Ice Cream Cookbook

Equipment

High Speed Blender

Mixing bowl

Ice cream container

INGREDIENTS

- 1-1/2 cup plant milk
- 2 tbsp oats (gluten-free if needed)
- 1 tsp. coffee
- 3-4 dates
- 1 tbsp. coconut sugar
- 2 tbsps. cacao powder
- 1 tsp ground coffee
- 1 oz. vegan dark chocolate
- 1 tsp vanilla extract
- Pinch of salt

DIRECTIONS

1. Add plant-based milk in cooking pan with oat and cook on medium heat.
2. Simmer mixture on low heat for about 12-15 minutes until oat become tender and mixture is thick.
3. Remove mixture from heat and let it cool on room temperature.

Wilson K. Lee

4. Pour mixture in high speed blender and blend with all other ingredients until all ingredients are well incorporated.
5. If you are making ice cream without ice cream maker then freeze ice cream container for 24 hours.
6. Pour the mixture in ice cream container and place in the refrigerator for about 2 hours until the mixture reaches 40 degrees F or below.
7. Alternatively, pour the mixture into an ice cream maker and run maker according to manufacture instructions until required consistency reach.
8. Serve scoop of gelato in bowl with chocolate syrup on top.
9. Serve and enjoy!

NUTRITIONAL INFORMATION

Calories Per Servings, 71 kcal, 3 g Fat, 9 g Total Carbs, 7.6 g Fiber, 1 g Protein

The Home Kitchen Ice Cream Cookbook

Vegan Maple Vanilla Gelato

Don't have any vegan chocolate or alternatives handy? This recipe is easy to make with the ingredients already in your kitchen!

Prep Time   10Min

Cooking time 15 Min

Total Time   25 Min

Servings   6

Equipment

High Speed Blender

Wilson K. Lee

Mixing bowl

Ice cream container

Cooking pan

INGREDIENTS

- 1-1/2 cup plant milk
- 2 tbsp oats (gluten-free if needed)
- 1/2 cup cashews (soaked overnight)
- 1/4 cup maple syrup
- 1 tsp vanilla extract
- Pinch of salt
- 1 tsp. coffee

DIRECTIONS

1. Add plant-based milk in cooking pan with oat and cook on medium heat.
2. Simmer mixture on low heat for about 12-15 minutes until oat become tender and mixture is thick.
3. Remove mixture from heat and let it cool on room temperature.
4. Pour mixture in high speed blender and blend with all other ingredients until all ingredients are well incorporated.

The Home Kitchen Ice Cream Cookbook

5. If you are making ice cream without ice cream maker then freeze ice cream container for 24 hours.

6. Pour the mixture in ice cream container and place in the refrigerator for about 2 hours until the mixture reaches 40 degrees F or below.

7. Alternatively, pour the mixture into an ice cream maker and run maker according to manufacture instructions until required consistency reach.

8. Serve scoop of gelato in bowl with maple syrup on top.

9. Serve and enjoy!

NUTRITIONAL INFORMATION

Calories Per Servings, 190 kcal, 12 g Fat18 g Total Carbs, 7.6 g Fibre, 3 g Protein

Wilson K. Lee

Chapter 4 - Delicious Sherbet Recipes

Coconut Orange Sherbet

Fresh orange juice and coconut water, make a healthy and nutritious sherbet recipe. Dairy free and easy to make in summer for a refreshing treat to beat the heat.

Prep Time   15 Min

Servings   4

Equipment

High Speed Blender

The Home Kitchen Ice Cream Cookbook

Mixing bowl

Ice cream Maker

INGREDIENTS

- 7 oz. white sugar
- 1 1/2 tablespoons finely grated orange zest
- 1/4 teaspoon kosher salt
- 2 cups freshly squeezed orange juice,
- 1 tablespoon freshly squeezed lemon juice
- 1 teaspoon vanilla extract
- 1 1/2 cups coconut water

DIRECTIONS

1. Add all ingredients in food processor except coconut water and blend until all ingredients and sugar dissolved and well mixed.
2. Transfer the mixture to a mixing bowl and add in coconut water.
3. Cover the bowl and place in the refrigerator for about 2 hours until the mixture reaches 40 degrees F or below.
4. If you are making ice cream without ice cream maker then freeze ice cream container for 24 hours.

Wilson K. Lee

5. Pour the mixture into an ice cream maker and run maker according to manufacture instructions until required consistency reach.

6. You can serve as it or can freeze again in ice cream molds until firm.

7. Serve and enjoy!

NUTRITIONAL INFORMATION

Calories Per Servings, 278 kcal, 1 g Fat, 18 g Total Carbs, 7.6 g Fiber, 1 g Protein

Coconut Lime Sherbet

All out of oranges? This lime sherbet recipe is also dairy free and another great refreshing citrus snack!

Prep Time   15 Min

Servings   4

Equipment

High Speed Blender

Mixing bowl

Ice cream container

Wilson K. Lee

INGREDIENTS

- 2 teaspoons lime zest
- 1/2 cup lime juice
- 1 cup coconut water
- 1/2 cup sugar
- Lime slice

DIRECTIONS

1. Mix together lime zest and lime juice with coconut water and sugar.
2. If you are making ice cream without ice cream maker then freeze ice cream container for 24 hours Pour mixture in ice cream molds with lime slice and freeze in freezer 4 hours or overnight.
3. Once sherbet is firm and hard, remove from freezer.
4. Serve and enjoy in summer.

NUTRITIONAL INFORMATION

Calories Per Servings, 68 kcal, 17.93 g Fat, 17 g Total Carbs, 1 g Fibre, 1 g Protein

The Home Kitchen Ice Cream Cookbook

Peach Sherbet with Cherries

The perfect way to eat fruits in the summer, fresh peaches are mixed with coconut water for dairy free fun. This dessert is best served with cranberries and waffle crunches.

Prep Time   20 Min

Servings   6

Equipment

High Speed Blender

Mixing bowl

Wilson K. Lee

Ice cream container

INGREDIENTS

- 16 oz. frozen peaches
- 1 can condensed milk
- 2 cup coconut water
- Fresh cherries for serving
- Waffle chunks for serving

DIRECTIONS

1. Add frozen peaches, water and milk in food processor or electric blender and blend for 2-3 minutes until mixture become creamy and fluffy.
2. Serve immediately as it is.
3. If you are making ice cream without ice cream maker then freeze ice cream container for 24 hours.
4. Pour sherbet in an ice cream container, and freeze for at least 3-4 hours to set and harden.
5. Pour scoops of sherbet over waffle chunks and top with fresh berries.
6. Serve and enjoy!!

NUTRITIONAL INFORMATION

The Home Kitchen Ice Cream Cookbook

Calories Per Servings, 144 kcal, 2 g Fat, 28 g Total Carbs, 7.6 g Fibre, 2 g Protein

Wilson K. Lee

Strawberry Coconut Sherbet

Sweet summer strawberries blended with coconut water, coconut flour and lemon juice, a healthy and nutritious sherbet recipe. This recipe is great for family members of all ages.

Prep Time   45 Min

Servings   4

Equipment

High Speed Blender

Mixing bowl

The Home Kitchen Ice Cream Cookbook

Ice cream container

INGREDIENTS

- 1 lb. strawberries, washed and hulled
- ¾ cup sugar
- 1 tablespoon lemon juice
- 1 ½ cup coconut milk
- 1 oz. coconut flour

DIRECTIONS

1. Add strawberries, sugar and lemon juice in high speed blender, until smooth and liquid.
2. Strain strawberries with strainer and discard seeds and strawberry pulp.
3. Add coconut milk and coconut flour to strawberry juice and mix well.
4. If you are making ice cream without ice cream maker then freeze ice cream container for 24 hours.
5. Pour mixture in ice cream container and freeze for 2-4 hours.
6. Once sherbet is hardening and set, remove from freezer.
7. Serve with strawberry slice and enjoy in summer.

Wilson K. Lee

NUTRITIONAL INFORMATION

Calories Per Servings, 318 kcal, 21 g Fat, 32 g Total Carbs, 7.6 g Fibre, 2 g Protein

The Home Kitchen Ice Cream Cookbook

Lemon Buttermilk Sherbet

This sherbet is made with lemon juice and buttermilk, but don't worry, it won't curdle! It provides just the right amount of tang and a creamier texture than dairy free versions.

Prep Time   15Min

Servings   4

Equipment

Wilson K. Lee

High Speed Blender

Mixing bowl

Ice cream container

INGREDIENTS

- 1 cup granulated sugar
- 3/4 cup water
- 3 tablespoons packed, coarsely chopped lemon verbena
- 2 1/2 cups cold buttermilk
- 1 tablespoon grated lemon rind
- Dash of salt Lemon rind strips

DIRECTIONS

1. Add sugar water and lemon verbena in a saucepan and heat over medium heat.
2. Stir and cook for 4-5 minutes until sugar is dissolved.
3. Bring the sugar mixture to a boil for 2-3 minutes.
4. Remove sugar mixture from heat and let it cool on room temperature.
5. Strain sugar syrup with strainer.
6. Add buttermilk, lemon rind, and salt in sugar syrup.
7. If you are making ice cream without ice cream maker then freeze ice cream molds for 24 hours.
8. Spoon sherbet into an ice cream molds and freeze for 2-4 hours until set and harden.

9. Serve and enjoy!

NUTRITIONAL INFORMATION

Calories Per Servings, 165 kcal, 1 g Fat, 34 g Total Carbs, 7.6 g Fibre, 5 g Protein

Wilson K. Lee

Coconut Pineapple Sherbet

Pina Coladas anyone? While you can add a bit of alcohol for a festive adult version, the virgin recipe below is great for family pool parties or days at the beach.

Prep Time   15 Min

Servings   4

Equipment

High Speed Blender

Mixing bowl

Ice cream container

The Home Kitchen Ice Cream Cookbook

INGREDIENTS

- 1 large lemon juice
- 1 tsp. lemon zest
- 2cups granulated sugar
- 1 quart half-and-half
- 1 can crushed pineapple in juice
- 1 oz. coconut flour

DIRECTIONS

1. Dissolve sugar with 1 cup water in small pan over medium heat.
2. Remove from heat and set aside.
3. Once sugar syrup is cool, add lemon juice pineapple juice with pineapple and coconut.
4. Pour all ingredients in blender and blend until smooth puree form.
5. If you are making ice cream without ice cream maker then freeze ice cream container for 24 hours.
6. Pour mixture in ice cream container and freeze for 1 hour.
7. Spoon the partially frozen mixture into serving bowl and freeze again for 2-4 hours until set.
8. Once sherbet is set remove from freezer.
9. Drizzle coconut flour on top.
10. Serve and enjoy!

Wilson K. Lee

NUTRITIONAL INFORMATION

Calories Per Servings, 295 kcal, 1 g Fat, 74 g Total Carbs, 7.6 g Fibre, 8 g Protein

The Home Kitchen Ice Cream Cookbook

Cocoa Cherry Sherbet

Leftover cranberries from holiday festivities? No worries, this recipe is great for enjoying while you're cozying up next to the fire.

Prep Time   15Min

Servings   4

Equipment

High Speed Blender

Mixing bowl

Ice cream container

Wilson K. Lee

INGREDIENTS

- 2 cups frozen sweet cherries (juice included) or 3 cups very ripe pitted fresh sweet cherries
- 1 cup sugar
- 1 1/2 cups coconut water
- ½ tsp. cocoa powder
- 2 tablespoons kirsch or other cherry liquor
- 1/4 cup fresh lemon juice

DIRECTIONS

1. Pour cherries in a small saucepan with water over medium-high heat until bring to boil.
2. Stir and cook on low heat for 5-10 minutes until cherries are soft and their juice is released.
3. Pour cherry mixture to a high-speed blender and blend for 1 minute.
4. Strain mixture through strainer and extract juice.
5. Remove seeds and cherries puree and discard them.
6. Add sugar to Cherrie juice and mix until sugar has dissolved completely.
7. Let it cool on room temperature for 1 hour.
8. Add cocoa powder, coconut water, kirsch, and lemon juice and mix well.

The Home Kitchen Ice Cream Cookbook

9. If you are making ice cream without ice cream maker then freeze ice cream container for 24 hours.

10. Pour mixture into ice cream molds and freeze for 2-4 hours until firm and set.

11. Once set remove molds from freezer.

12. Drizzle coconut flour on top.

13. Serve and enjoy!

NUTRITIONAL INFORMATION

Calories Per Servings, 295 kcal, 1 g Fat, 74 g Total Carbs, 7.6 g Fibre, 1 g Protein

Wilson K. Lee

Avocado-Basil Sherbet

Another great option with healthy avocado and refreshing basil, this recipe offers another texture option with coconut and lemongrass.

Prep Time   15 Min

Servings   4

Equipment

The Home Kitchen Ice Cream Cookbook

High Speed Blender

Mixing bowl

Ice cream container

INGREDIENTS

- 3 cups coconut water
- 1 cup lemongrass
- 1 cup heavy cream
- 3/4 cup fresh basil leaves
- 2/3 cup sugar
- 1 avocado, chopped
- 2 tablespoons light corn syrup
- 1/2 teaspoon kosher salt

DIRECTIONS

1. Heat water, lemongrass, and cream in a large saucepan over medium heat and boil for 4-5 minutes.
2. Remove from heat and let it stand on kitchen counter for 20 minutes.
3. Strain cream mixture through strainer and discard lemon grass.

4. Add basil, avocado, sugar, cream mixture corn syrup, and salt to blender and blend on high speed until all ingredients well incorporated.
5. Purée on high speed until well blended, about 1 minute.
6. Strain mixture again through a strainer.
7. If you are making ice cream without ice cream maker then freeze ice cream container for 24 hours.
8. Pour mixture in ice cream container and freeze for 4 hours.
9. Serve scoops of sherbet in bowl with basil leaves.
10. Enjoy!

NUTRITIONAL INFORMATION

Calories Per Servings, 314 kcal, 18 g Fat, 36 g Total Carbs, 7.6 g Fibre, 2 g Protein

Cantaloupe Sherbet

Fresh cantaloupe melon is so juicy and refreshing. It's also a great neutral flavor to pair with soda for a great summer punch!

Prep Time   15 Min

Servings   4

Equipment

High Speed Blender

Wilson K. Lee

Mixing bowl

Ice cream container

INGREDIENTS

- 1 large ripe cantaloupe, peeled and finely chopped
- 1/3 cup sweetener
- 2 tablespoons lemon juice
- 2 teaspoons unflavored gelatin
- 1/4 cup cold water
- 1 can vanilla fat-free yogurt
- Cantaloupe wedge

DIRECTIONS

1. Blend cantaloupe, sweetener, and lemon juice in a blender and blend on high speed until all ingredients are smooth and creamy.
2. Pour mixture in medium size bowl
3. until smooth. Transfer mixture to a medium bowl.
4. Mix gelatin powder with hot water in pan and let it stand for 1 minute.
5. Add gelatin and rest of the ingredients to cantaloupe mixture and mix well.
6. If you are making ice cream without ice cream maker then freeze ice cream container for 24 hours.

The Home Kitchen Ice Cream Cookbook

7. Pour mixture in ice cream container and freeze for 4 hours until set and firm.

8. Transfer mixture to a large bowl; beat with a mixer at high speed until fluffy. Spoon mixture back into pan; freeze until firm.

9. Scoop mixture into 4-5 serving bowls.

10. into 5 individual serving dishes to serve. Serve with cantaloupe slice and enjoy!

NUTRITIONAL INFORMATION

Calories Per Servings, 433 kcal, 17.93 g Fat, 63.99 g Total Carbs, 7.6 g Fibre, 9.59 g Protein

Wilson K. Lee

Simple Banana Sherbet

Leftover bananas? This sherbet recipe will go great with the banana bread you're also already probably planning to make!

Prep Time   15 Min

Servings   4

Equipment

High Speed Blender

Mixing bowl

The Home Kitchen Ice Cream Cookbook

Ice cream container

INGREDIENTS

- 4 bananas
- 2/3 cup coconut sugar
- 2 cups coconut water
- 1/8 tsp kosher salt
- 1 tsp vanilla extract
- 1 cup sour cream

DIRECTIONS

1. Pour banana, sugar and water in high speed blender and blend on high speed. Blend on high until the mixture is smooth and creamy
2. Add salt, vanilla extract and sour cream in banana mixture and blend again.
3. If you are making ice cream without ice cream maker then freeze ice cream container for 24 hours.
4. Pour banana sherbet mix into an ice cream container and freeze for 4 hours until set and firm.
5. Once sherbet is set remove from freezer.
6. Serve scoops of sherbet in bowls.
7. Enjoy!

NUTRITIONAL INFORMATION

Wilson K. Lee

Calories Per Servings, 433 kcal, 17.93 g Fat, 63.99 g Total Carbs, 7.6 g Fibre, 9.59 g Protein

The Home Kitchen Ice Cream Cookbook

Coconut Chocolate Sorbet

Just like Mounds candy, coconut and chocolate are a match made in heaven. Add in some almonds for another layer of flavor and a fun healthy crunch!

Prep Time   10 Min

Cooking Time 10 Min

Servings   4

Equipment

Wilson K. Lee

High Speed Blender

Mixing bowl

Ice cream container

Cooking pan

Ice cream Maker

INGREDIENTS

- 1/4 cups coconut water
- 1 cup coconut sugar
- Pinch of salt
- 3/4 cup unsweetened cocoa powder
- 6 oz. chocolate, chopped
- 1/2 teaspoon vanilla extract

DIRECTIONS

1. Heat coconut water, sugar, salt, and cocoa powder over medium heat in medium sauce pan.
2. Bring the mixture to boil over medium heat.
3. Stir and simmer for 10 minutes.
4. Remove chocolate mixture from heat and add the chocolate, vanilla and mix well.
5. Taste and adjust sweetener according to taste.

The Home Kitchen Ice Cream Cookbook

6. If you are making ice cream without ice cream maker then freeze ice cream container for 24 hours.
7. Pour mixture in ice cream molds and freeze for 4 hours or until set and firm.
8. Serve and enjoy!

NUTRITIONAL INFORMATION

Calories Per Servings, 123 kcal, 17.93 g Fat, 63.99 g Total Carbs, 7.6 g Fibre, 9.59 g Protein

Wilson K. Lee

Creamy Mint Sherbet

There's nothing like fresh mint. This recipe combines the refreshing herb with additional spices for a uniquely spicy cooling treat that your guests won't soon forget!

Prep Time   15Min

Servings   4

Equipment

High Speed Blender

Mixing bowl

Ice cream container

The Home Kitchen Ice Cream Cookbook

Cooking pan

Ice cream Maker

INGREDIENTS

- 1 1/4 cups granulated sugar
- 1 cup water
- 1 bunch mint leaves
- 3 1/4-inch coins fresh ginger root
- 5 whole peppercorns
- 4 whole cardamom pods, cracked or 1/8 teaspoon ground
- 1/8 teaspoon ground nutmeg
- 1 cinnamon stick
- Generous pinch fine sea salt
- 1 1/2 cups plain yogurt

DIRECTIONS

1. Dissolve sugar and water in a large saucepan over high heat.
2. Stir and cook until the sugar completely dissolves in water.
3. Once mixture boiled, remove from heat.

Wilson K. Lee

4. Add the mint leaves, ginger, peppercorns, cardamom, and other spice in sugar syrup and let it stand covered for 10 minutes.
5. Strain the mixture through strainer and discard spices.
6. Pour yogurt in sugar syrup and mix well.
7. If you are making ice cream without ice cream maker then freeze ice cream container for 24 hours.
8. Pour mixture in ice cream container and freeze for 4 hours or until set and firm.
9. Serve and enjoy!

NUTRITIONAL INFORMATION

Calories Per Servings, 265 kcal, 1 g Fat, 15 g Total Carbs, 7.6 g Fibre, 2 g Protein

The Home Kitchen Ice Cream Cookbook

Greek Yogurt & Chia Sherbet

Greek yogurt is mixed with chia seeds for a healthy and nutritious sherbet recipe. Make ahead of time for quick summer breakfasts for the kids!

Prep Time   15 Min

Servings   2

Equipment

High Speed Blender

Ice cream container

Wilson K. Lee

Cooking pan

Ice cream Maker

INGREDIENTS

- 2 cups milk, divided
- 1 cup sugar
- 1 ¼ lb. Greek Yogurt
- 1 tbsps. chia seed
- ¾ teaspoon vanilla extract

DIRECTIONS

1. Dissolve sugar and milk in pan over medium heat.
2. Stir for 3-4 minutes over medium heat and bring mixture to boil.
3. Remove milk and sugar mixture from heat and let it cool on room temperature.
4. Add yogurt, chia seeds and vanilla in milk mixture and mix well.
5. If you are making ice cream without ice cream molds then freeze ice cream container for 24 hours.
6. Pour mixture in ice cream molds and freeze for 4 hours or until set and firm.
7. Serve and enjoy!

The Home Kitchen Ice Cream Cookbook

NUTRITIONAL INFORMATION

Calories Per Servings, 241 kcal, 17.93 g Fat, 63.99 g Total Carbs, 7.6 g Fibre, 9.59 g Protein

Wilson K. Lee

Coconut Milk Orange Sherbet

Tart and tangy orange balances with creamy coconut and vanilla for an authentic, healthier Creamsicle alternative!

Prep Time   15 Min

Servings   4

Equipment

High Speed Blender

Mixing bowl

Ice cream container

The Home Kitchen Ice Cream Cookbook

Cooking pan

Ice cream Maker

INGREDIENTS

- 2 cups orange juice
- 1 tbsp. lemon juice
- 1 cup cane juice
- ⅛ tsp sea salt
- ½ tsp vanilla extract
- 1¾ cup coconut milk, refrigerated overnight
- 2 tbsp. orange zest

DIRECTIONS

1. The night before making the sherbet, place the oranges and coconut milk in the refrigerator. Place the ice cream maker's freezer bowl in the freezer.
2. Add orange juice, lemon juice, sugar, salt, vanilla extract, and coconut milk in a high-speed blender and blend until the sugar is dissolved and all ingredients are well incorporated.
3. Strain the mixture with strainer and pour in bowl.
4. Add the orange zest in juice mixture and mix well.
5. If you are making ice cream without ice cream maker then freeze ice cream container for 24 hours.

187

Wilson K. Lee

6. Pour the mixture in ice cream molds and refrigerate until mixture is 40F or less.

7. Alternatively, pour mixture in an ice cream maker and process according to the manufacturer's directions.

8. Serve and enjoy or store sherbet in refrigerator for up to 2 weeks.

NUTRITIONAL INFORMATION

Calories Per Servings, 252 kcal, 17.93 g Fat, 63.99 g Total Carbs, 7.6 g Fibre, 9.59 g Protein

Mango Buttermilk Sherbet

All-time favorite mango is blended with buttermilk, lemon juice, sugar and vodka. Freeze in popsicle molds for convenient party consumption!

Prep Time   15 Min

Servings   10

Equipment

Wilson K. Lee

High Speed Blender

Mixing bowl

Ice cream container

Cooking pan

Ice cream Maker

INGREDIENTS

- 4 large mangoes peeled, pitted, and chopped
- 3/4 cup sugar
- 2 tbsp. vodka
- 2 cups buttermilk
- 1 tbsp. fresh lemon juice

DIRECTIONS

1. Add mangoes, sugar, vodka, and buttermilk and lemon juice into a food processor.
2. Blend food processor for 2-3 minutes on high speed until mixture is smooth and creamy.
3. Strain the mango mixture with strainer and press with wooden spoon to extract juice.
4. Discard the remaining solids and pulp of mixture from puree.

5. If you are making ice cream without ice cream maker then freeze ice cream container for 24 hours.
6. Pour the mixture in an ice cream maker and run maker according to the manufacturer's directions.
7. Alternatively, pour the mixture in ice cream molds and refrigerate until mixture is 40F or less

NUTRITIONAL INFORMATION

Calories Per Servings, 199 kcal, 17.93 g Fat, 63.99 g Total Carbs, 7.6 g Fibre, 9.59 g Protein

Wilson K. Lee

Avocado Sorbet

Just in case you weren't on board with our other avocado options, this sorbet is as simple as it gets!

Prep Time   15 Min

Servings   4

Equipment

High Speed Blender

Mixing bowl

Ice cream container

The Home Kitchen Ice Cream Cookbook

Ice cream Maker

INGREDIENTS

- 2/3 to 3/4 cup avocado, cut into chunks
- 1/2 cup agave syrup
- 1/2 cup light coconut milk
- 1/4 cup fresh lime juice
- 2 teaspoons finely grated lime zest

DIRECTIONS

1. Add avocado in high speed blender and blend until become smooth.
2. Add the agave syrup, and blend again for 30 seconds.
3. Slowly add the coconut milk, and blend again.
4. Add the lime juice and lime zest in avocado and milk mixture and process until all ingredients are well incorporated.
5. Transfer the sorbet mixture to ice cream container and freeze at least 4 hours to overnight.
6. If you are making ice cream without ice cream maker then freeze ice cream container for 24 hours.
7. Alternatively, pour the avocado sorbet mixture in an ice cream maker and process to reach required consistency.
8. Freeze again and serve.

Wilson K. Lee

9. Enjoy!

NUTRITIONAL INFORMATION

Calories Per Servings, 225 kcal, 17.93 g Fat, 63.99 g Total Carbs, 7.6 g Fibre, 9.59 g Protein

Blueberry Buttermilk Sherbet

This is a great way to repurpose some leftover frozen blueberries from summer. Buttermilk adds the creamy texture and balances the tartness.

Prep Time   15 Min

Servings   4

Equipment

High Speed Blender

Mixing bowl

Ice cream container

INGREDIENTS

Wilson K. Lee

- 3 cups fresh blueberries, or frozen, thawed
- 1 cup sugar
- 2 cups buttermilk, regular or low-fat
- 1 teaspoon pure vanilla extract

DIRECTIONS

1. Add blueberries in high speed blender and process for 1-2 minutes until smooth.
2. Strainer blueberry puree with strainer, press puree with wooden spoon.
3. Discard pulp and solids.
4. Blend sugar, buttermilk, and vanilla with blueberry juice in blender and mix well until sugar is dissolved.
5. If you are making ice cream without ice cream maker then freeze ice cream container for 24 hours.
6. Pour mixture into an ice cream molds and freeze for at least 4 hours to set and firm.
7. Serve and enjoy!

NUTRITIONAL INFORMATION

Calories Per Servings, 433 kcal, 17.93 g Fat, 63.99 g Total Carbs, 7.6 g Fibre, 9.59 g Protein

Coconut Green Apple Sorbet

Another great dairy free recipe! Green apple is a great flavor for autumn get togethers, especially if you live in a warmer climate.

Prep Time   15 Min

Servings   4

Equipment

High Speed Blender

Mixing bowl

Wilson K. Lee

Ice cream container

Cooking pan

Ice cream Maker

INGREDIENTS

- 1 cup granulated sugar
- 1 cup coconut water
- 3 green apples. Chopped
- 2 tbsps. Lemon juice
- 1 cup coconut water
- 1 egg white, lightly whisked

DIRECTIONS

1. Add sugar and water in small pan over medium heat.
2. Let the mixture simmer in a small saucepan over medium-high heat for 4-5 minutes.
3. Stir occasionally until the sugar is dissolved and syrup is thick.
4. Remove syrup from heat and let it cool on room temperature for 1 hour.
5. Meanwhile extract juice of green apple from juice machine.
6. Add lemon juice in apple juice and mix well.
7. If you do not have juicer them blend apples in blender and extract the juice through strainer.

The Home Kitchen Ice Cream Cookbook

8. Add coconut water, sugar syrup and the egg white in apple mixture.
9. If you are making ice cream without ice cream maker then freeze ice cream container for 24 hours.
10. Pour mixture in ice cream molds and freeze in freezer for 4 hours until set and firm.
11. Alternatively, pour mixture in ice cream maker and process following the manufacturer's instructions.
12. Serve and enjoy!

NUTRITIONAL INFORMATION

Calories Per Servings, 433 kcal, 17.93 g Fat, 63.99 g Total Carbs, 7.6 g Fibre, 9.59 g Protein

Wilson K. Lee

Coconut Cranberries Sherbet

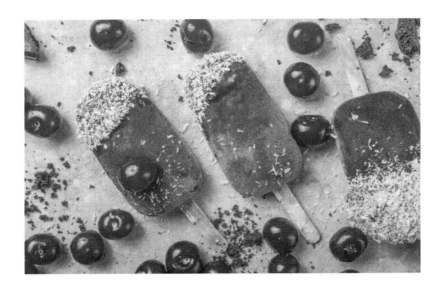

Here's the dairy free alternative to our coconut cranberry gelato for all your vegan & lactose sensitive loved ones!

Prep Time   15 Min

Servings   4

Equipment

High Speed Blender

Mixing bowl

Ice cream container

The Home Kitchen Ice Cream Cookbook

INGREDIENTS

- 2 cups cranberries
- 1 cup sugar
- 1 1/2 cups coconut water
- 1 oz coconut flakes
- 1/4 cup fresh lemon juice

DIRECTIONS

1. If you are making ice cream without ice cream maker then freeze ice cream container for 24 hours.
2. Pour berries in a small saucepan with water over medium-high heat until bring to boil.
3. Stir and cook on low heat for 5-10 minutes until cherries are soft and their juice is released.
4. Pour berries mixture to a high-speed blender and blend for 1 minute.
5. Strain mixture through strainer and extract juice.
6. Remove seeds and berries puree and discard them.
7. Add sugar and coconut flour to berries juice and mix until sugar has dissolved completely.
8. Let it cool on room temperature for 1 hour.
9. Add coconut water, and lemon juice and mix well.
10. Pour mixture into ice cream molds and freeze for 2-4 hours until firm and set.
11. Once set remove molds from freezer.

Wilson K. Lee

12. Drizzle coconut flour on top.

13. Serve and enjoy!

NUTRITIONAL INFORMATION

Calories Per Servings, 433 kcal, 17.93 g Fat, 63.99 g Total Carbs, 7.6 g Fibre, 9.59 g Protein

The Home Kitchen Ice Cream Cookbook

Melon Sherbet

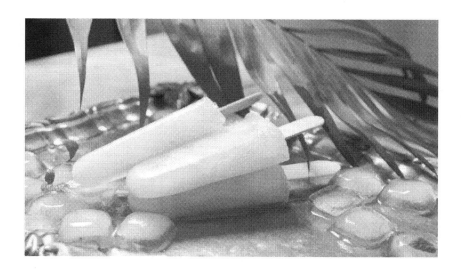

This four ingredient sherbet is great with any type of melon on hand! Also delicious as an edible ice cube in your favorite summer drink.

Prep Time   15 Min

Servings   4

Equipment

High Speed Blender

Mixing bowl

Ice cream container

Wilson K. Lee

INGREDIENTS

- 2 cups melon
- 1 cup sugar
- 1 1/2 cups coconut water
- 1/4 cup fresh lemon juice

DIRECTIONS

1. Pour all ingredients to a high-speed blender and blend for 1 minute.
2. Strain mixture through strainer and extract juice.
3. Remove seeds and melon puree and discard them.
4. If you are making ice cream without ice cream maker then freeze ice cream container for 24 hours.
5. Pour mixture into ice cream molds and freeze for 2-4 hours until firm and set.
6. Once set remove molds from freezer.
7. Serve and enjoy!

NUTRITIONAL INFORMATION

Calories Per Servings, 433 kcal, 17.93 g Fat, 63.99 g Total Carbs, 7.6 g Fibre, 9.59 g Protein

The Home Kitchen Ice Cream Cookbook

Chapter 5 - Low Carb Ice cream Recipes

Low Carb Chocolate Chip Ice Cream

Chocolate chip low carb ice cream is fluffy and creamy, and sugar free –great for people trying to lose weight. Serve a scoop with a bowl of berries for the perfect happy medium treat!

Prep Time   10Min

Cooking time 15 Min

Wilson K. Lee

Total Time   25 Min

Servings   6

Equipment

Mixing bowl

Ice cream container

Ice cream maker.

Cooking Pan

INGREDIENTS

- 3 cups heavy whipped cream
- 1/2 cup cacao powder
- 1/3 cup almond milk
- 4 large egg yolks
- 1 tbsp MCT oil
- 1.5 tsp powdered gelatin
- 2/3 cup powdered erythritol
- 1 tbsp vanilla extract sugar free
- 1/4 tsp. salt
- ½ cup sugar-free chocolate chips

DIRECTIONS.

The Home Kitchen Ice Cream Cookbook

1. Place the cacao powder and cream into a medium saucepan over medium heat.
2. Stir and mix well with wooden spoon until cacao powder in mixed.
3. Add milk and bring the mixture to simmer over medium heat.
4. Stir and cook for 4-5 minutes.
5. Beat egg yolks with powder erythritol in small pan with beater until smooth and fluffy.
6. Slowly add beaten eggs in cream mixture and mix well until all ingredients are mix together.
7. Mix gelatin in a small bowl with 1 tbsp of water and let it stand for 5 minutes.
8. Add gelatin mix in pan mixture and mix with wooden spoon.
9. Mixture should be thick enough to coat over spoon.
10. Add the vanilla and MCT oil in cream mixture and let it stand at room temperature for 30 minutes.
11. If you are making ice cream without ice cream maker then freeze ice cream container for 24 hours.
12. Spoon mixture into ice cream container and carefully chocolate chips in mixture.
13. Freeze mixture in freezer for 2-4 hours until set and firm.

Wilson K. Lee

14. Alternatively, pour the chocolate mixture into the ice cream maker and churn for 40 Serve scoops in serving bowl.
15. Enjoy!

NUTRITIONAL INFORMATION

Calories Per Servings, 325 kcal, 17.93 g Fat, 15 g Total Carbs, 7.6 g Fibre, 9.59 g Protein

Low Carb Vanilla Ice Cream

This easy-egg free vanilla ice cream is low carb, fluffy, and sugar free. Delicious with a fresh waffle and fruit for a fun weekend treat!

Prep Time   10Min

Cooking time 15 Min

Total Time   25 Min

Servings   6

Equipment

Wilson K. Lee

Mixing bowl

Ice cream container

Ice cream maker.

Cooking Pan

INGREDIENTS

- 2 cups heavy whipping cream
- 2 cups coconut milk
- ¾ cup Splenda
- 2 tsp vanilla extract
- Waffle for serving
- Caramel for topping
- Fresh Berries for topping

DIRECTIONS

1. Beat all ingredients in small mixing bowl on low to high speed for 4-5 minutes until all ingredients are blended together.
2. If you are making ice cream without ice cream maker then freeze ice cream container for 24 hours.
3. Pour mixture in ice cream container and freeze for 1 hour.
4. Take mixture from freezer and blend in blender.

The Home Kitchen Ice Cream Cookbook

5. Return the ice cream to the freezer and freeze again.
6. Perform this task until your ice cream has desired consistency.
7. Freeze ice cream for 8 hours until firm and set.
8. Scoop ice cream over waffle.
9. Top with fresh berries and caramel.
10. Serve and enjoy!

NUTRITIONAL INFORMATION

Calories Per Servings, 342 kcal, 17.93 g Fat, 13 g Total Carbs, 7.6 g Fibre, 9.59 g Protein

Wilson K. Lee

Raspberry Rich Chocolate Ice Cream

This raspberry rich chocolate, low carb ice cream is fluffy, creamy, and sugar free. The cream cheese adds a cheesecake-like texture and unique flavor profile.

Prep Time   10Min

Cooking time 15 Min

Total Time   25 Min

Servings   6

Equipment

Mixing bowl

The Home Kitchen Ice Cream Cookbook

Ice cream container

Ice cream maker.

Cooking Pan

INGREDIENTS

- 6 egg yolks
- 4 oz erythritol
- 2-1/2 cup heavy cream
- 1 cup raspberries
- 1 cup cream cheese
- 1 tsp vanilla extract
- 3 tbsps. Unsweetened cocoa powder

DIRECTIONS

1. Heat the heavy cream and vanilla in a saucepan over low heat for 1-2 minutes.
2. Remove from heat and let it cool for few minutes on room temperature.
3. Beat egg yolks with the erythritol with electric beater until mixture is smooth.
4. Add cocoa powder and mix well.
5. Slowly add egg mixture in cream mixture and mix well.
6. Heat and cook again on low heat for 2-3 minutes.

Wilson K. Lee

7. Stir and cook until mixture thick enough to coat on spoon.
8. Once mixture is thick remove from heat and let it cool on room temperature.
9. Add in cream cheese and raspberries and blend in high speed blender for 2 minutes.
10. If you are making ice cream without ice cream maker then freeze ice cream container for 24 hours.
11. Pour the custard into ice cream container and freeze for 4 -6 hours.
12. Alternatively, pour the mixture into your ice cream churner and let the machine to churn.
13. Serve with fresh raspberries and enjoy!

NUTRITIONAL INFORMATION

Calories Per Servings, 300 kcal, 17.93 g Fat, 12 g Total Carbs, 7.6 g Fibre, 9.59 g Protein

Oreo Ice Cream

You'll never buy store bought again after you try this great low carb alternative! Oreo biscuits are crumbled with cream cheese for that great cookie flavor.

Prep Time   10Min

Cooking time 15 Min

Total Time   25 Min

Servings   6

Equipment

Mixing bowl

Wilson K. Lee

Ice cream container

Ice cream maker.

Cooking Pan

INGREDIENTS

- 1 cup frozen cream cheese
- 1/2 cup frozen heavy cream
- 1/2 cup frozen coconut cream
- 6 low carb Oreo biscuits
- 1/8 tsp stevia powder

DIRECTIONS

1. Blend cream cheese, heavy cream, heavy cream, stevia and coconut cream in blender for 1-2 minutes.
2. Pour mixture in bowl.
3. Crush Oreo biscuits in bowl with sharp knife.
4. Carefully fold in crushed Oreo in cream mixture.
5. If you are making ice cream without ice cream maker then freeze ice cream container for 24 hours.
6. Freeze again or serve immediately with waffle and Oreo biscuits on top.
7. Enjoy!

NUTRITIONAL INFORMATION

The Home Kitchen Ice Cream Cookbook

Calories Per Servings, 219 kcal, 17.93 g Fat, 3 g Total Carbs, 7.6 g Fibre, 9.59 g Protein

Wilson K. Lee

Cheesecake Ice Cream

Cheesecake AND ice cream? Truly the best of both worlds. And with only four ingredients, it couldn't be easier.

Prep Time   15 Min

Servings   6

Equipment

Mixing bowl

Ice cream container

Ice cream maker.

The Home Kitchen Ice Cream Cookbook

Cooking Pan

INGREDIENTS

- 2 cups cream cheese
- 1 cup heavy cream
- 3/4 cup of frozen unsweetened berries
- 3 teaspoons sweetener

DIRECTIONS

1. Crush fresh berries in small bowl and set aside.
2. Mix cream cheese, cream and sweetener in bowl and mix well.
3. Carefully fold in crushed berries.
4. If you are making ice cream without ice cream maker then freeze ice cream container for 24 hours.
5. Pour mixture in Ice cream container and freeze for 4-6 hours until set.
6. Serve scoops of ice cream in bowl with fresh berries on top.
7. Enjoy!

NUTRITIONAL INFORMATION

Calories Per Servings, 343 kcal, 17.93 g Fat, 10 g Total Carbs, 7.6 g Fibre, 9.59 g Protein

Wilson K. Lee

Blackberry Buttermilk Ice Cream

Similar to our blueberry buttermilk recipe, this blackberry alternative is great for more of a tart flavor and calls for lots of yummy spices for a more advanced flavor profile.

Prep Time   15 Min

Servings   4

Equipment

Mixing bowl

Ice cream container

Ice cream maker.

The Home Kitchen Ice Cream Cookbook

Cooking Pan

INGREDIENTS

- 1/2 lb. blackberries
- 2 tablespoons lemon juice
- 1 tablespoon water
- 1/8 teaspoon cinnamon
- 1 pinch freshly ground nutmeg
- 1/8 teaspoon almond extract
- 1/4 teaspoon vanilla extract
- 1/8 teaspoon stevia
- 1/4 cup balsamic vinegar
- 1 1/2 cups heavy cream
- 1 1/8 cups buttermilk
- 1/3 cup low carb sugar
- 2 tablespoons vanilla flavored vodka
- 1/4 teaspoon salt
- 1/2 teaspoon stevia glycerite

DIRECTIONS

1. Pour all ingredients in blender and blend to make a smooth paste.

Wilson K. Lee

2. If you are making ice cream without ice cream maker then freeze ice cream container for 24 hours.
3. Pour mixture in Ice cream container and freeze for 4-6 hours until set.
4. Serve scoops of ice cream in bowl with fresh berries on top.
5. Enjoy!

NUTRITIONAL INFORMATION

Calories Per Servings, 271 kcal, 17.93 g Fat, 12 g Total Carbs, 7.6 g Fibre, 4 g Protein

The Home Kitchen Ice Cream Cookbook

Quick Coffee Ice Cream

Prepped in just 15 minutes this 5 ingredient coffee ice cream is perfect for those caffeine lovers on the go!

Prep Time   15 Min

Servings   2

Equipment

Mixing bowl

Ice cream container

Ice cream maker.

Wilson K. Lee

Cooking Pan

INGREDIENTS

- 1 cup heavy whipping cream
- 1 serving instant coffee
- 1-1/2 tablespoon Swerve
- 1 teaspoon vanilla extract
- Low carb chocolate syrup

DIRECTIONS

1. Pour all ingredients into mixing bowl and mix well.
2. If you are making ice cream without ice cream maker then freeze ice cream container for 24 hours.
3. Pour mixture in ice cream container and freeze for 4-6 hours.
4. Pour scoop of ice cream in serving cup.
5. Drizzle chocolate syrup on top.
6. Serve and enjoy!

NUTRITIONAL INFORMATION

Calories Per Servings, 215 kcal, 17.93 g Fat, 2 g Total Carbs, 7.6 g Fibre, 9.59 g Protein

The Home Kitchen Ice Cream Cookbook

Ice Cream with Chocolate Flake

A great low-carb variation on the classic Stracciatella, this is a quick and easy treat that's sure to satisfy your pickiest of critics.

Prep Time   15 Min

Servings   8

Equipment

Mixing bowl

Wilson K. Lee

Ice cream container

Ice cream maker.

Cooking Pan

INGREDIENTS

- 3 cups heavy cream
- 1 1/2 cups almond milk
- 1 1/2 cups of powdered erythritol
- 2 tbsps. vanilla
- Pinch of salt
- 3/4 cup of dark sugar free chocolate
- 4 tbsps. of coconut oil

DIRECTIONS

1. Beat cream almond milk, powdered erythritol and salt in bowl with beater until well incorporated.
2. Alternatively,, you can blend above ingredients in blender.
3. If you are making ice cream without ice cream maker then freeze ice cream container for 24 hours.
4. Pour mixture in container and freeze for 4 hours, mix base after every 30 minutes with spoon.

The Home Kitchen Ice Cream Cookbook

5. Remove ice cream from ice cream maker and carefully fold in crushed chocolate in cream with coconut oil.
6. Freeze again in freezer and serve with chocolate on top.
7. Melt chocolate and coconut oil in oven and drizzle on top.
8. Enjoy!

NUTRITIONAL INFORMATION

Calories Per Servings, 230 kcal, 17.93 g Fat, 16 g Total Carbs, 7.6 g Fibre, 9.59 g Protein

Wilson K. Lee

Mint Chocolate Chip Ice Cream

A personal favorite, this is an egg free, low-carb take on a classic! The perfect combo of refreshing mint and rich dark chocolate is unforgettable.

Prep Time   10Min

Cooking time 15 Min

Total Time   25 Min

Servings   6

Equipment

The Home Kitchen Ice Cream Cookbook

Mixing bowl

Ice cream container

Ice cream maker.

Cooking Pan

INGREDIENTS

- 3/4 cup coconut milk
- 1-1/2 cups heavy cream
- 2/3 cup Swerve
- pinch salt
- 3/4 teaspoon mint extract
- 3/4 teaspoon peppermint extract
- 3/4 cup chopped mini semisweet chocolate chips
- 3/4 tbsp Knox unflavored gelatin

DIRECTIONS

1. Mix gelatin with milk and let it stand for 5 minutes.
2. Mix milk, cream, sweetener, salt, vanilla, mint extract in large bowl until sweetener is dissolved.
3. You can add some green food color in cream mixture.
4. If you are making ice cream without ice cream maker then freeze ice cream container for 24 hours.
5. Pour mixture in container and chill at least 2 hours.

Wilson K. Lee

6. Once the ice cream is set, carefully fold chocolate chips and mix well.
7. Freeze again for 4hours or overnight to set.
8. Alternatively, churn mixture in an ice cream machine according to manufacturers' instructions.
9. Serve scoop of ice cream in serving bowl with some chocolate chips on top and enjoy.

NUTRITIONAL INFORMATION

Calories Per Servings, 243 kcal, 18 g Fat, 15 g Total Carbs, 7.6 g Fibre, 3 g Protein

Coconut Chip Ice Cream

This recipe is made with cream, coconut flakes and cashew milk, served with chocolate chip cookies and is another great homemade recipe made without an ice cream machine.

Prep Time   10Min

Cooking time 15 Min

Total Time   25 Min

Servings   6

Equipment

Mixing bowl

Wilson K. Lee

Ice cream container

Ice cream maker.

Cooking Pan

INGREDIENTS

- ½ cup low carb chocolate chips
- ½ tbsp butter
- 2 ¼ cups cashew milk or low carb milk alternative
- 2 ¼ cups heavy whipping cream
- 1 cup powdered sugar
- 1 tbsp vanilla extract
- ½ tbsp coconut extract
- ¾ cup unsweetened coconut flakes
- Chocolate chip biscuits for serving

DIRECTIONS

1. Melt butter in pan over medium heat and add chocolate chips.
2. Remove from heat and set aside.
3. Mix the milk, cream, sweetener, vanilla, and coconut extract in large bowl until all ingredients are mix and sweetener is dissolved.
4. Add coconut flaxes in cream mixture and mix well.

The Home Kitchen Ice Cream Cookbook

5. If you are making ice cream without ice cream maker then freeze ice cream container for 24 hours.
6. Churn ice cream in ice cream maker for 20 minutes.
7. Alternatively, pour ice cream in container and freeze for 1 hour mix well.
8. Freeze for another 1 hour and mix again.
9. Finally, carefully fold in chocolate chips and freeze again for 4 hours until ice cream is set.
10. Once ice cream is set and firm, remove from freezer.
11. Serve scoop of ice cream between two chocolate chip cookies.
12. Enjoy

NUTRITIONAL INFORMATION

Calories Per Servings, 347 kcal, 22 g Fat, 12 g Total Carbs, 7.6 g Fibre, 4 g Protein

Wilson K. Lee

Cinnamon Ice Cream

A low carb holiday treat, this cinnamon ice cream is a great spiced option that can be made boozy for more fun festivities!

Prep Time   10Min

Cooking time 15 Min

Total Time   25 Min

Servings   6

Equipment

Mixing bowl

The Home Kitchen Ice Cream Cookbook

Ice cream container

Ice cream maker.

Cooking Pan

INGREDIENTS

- 2 cup cream heavy/whipping
- 1 cup coconut milk tinned
- 3 egg yolks
- 1/2 cup erythritol
- 1 tablespoon cinnamon ground
- 1 shot vodka optional
- 2 oz. chocolate, chopped

DIRECTIONS

1. Add cream and coconut milk in cooking pan over medium low heat.
2. Cook and stir for 2-4 minutes.
3. Beat eggs and erythritol together with electric beater in small pan.
4. Slowly add eggs in cream and mix well to avoid any lumps.
5. Mix until eggs are well incorporated.

Wilson K. Lee

6. Add cinnamon in cream, cook and stir for 5-10 minutes until mixture start to thicken.
7. Once mixture is thickened enough to coat over spoon, remove from heat.
8. Add vodka in cream mixture and mix again.
9. If you are making ice cream without ice cream maker then freeze ice cream container for 24 hours
10. Pour mixture in container and freeze for 4 hours, mix base after every 30 minutes with spoon.
11. Remove ice cream from freezer and carefully fold in crushed chocolate in cream.
12. Freeze again in freezer.
13. Serve and enjoy!

NUTRITIONAL INFORMATION

Calories Per Servings, 220 kcal, 18 g Fat, 10 g Total Carbs, 7.6 g Fibre, 3 g Protein

The Home Kitchen Ice Cream Cookbook

Coconut Caramel Ice Cream

In my opinion, coconut & caramel is a highly underrated flavor combination. Find out why with this simple low-carb recipe!

Prep Time   10Min

Cooking time 15 Min

Total Time   25 Min

Servings   6

Equipment

Mixing bowl

Wilson K. Lee

Ice cream container

Ice cream maker.

Cooking Pan

INGREDIENTS

- Caramel sauce
  - 1/4 cup butter
  - 1/4 cup brown erythritol
  - 1/2 cup heavy cream
- Ice Cream Base
  - 2 cups heavy cream
  - 1/2 cup allulose
  - 1 cup coconut, shredded or unsweetened desiccated coconut
  - 1/2 cup caramel sauce as per above

DIRECTIONS

1. Heat cooking pan over medium heat and melt the butter for 3-4 minutes.
2. Stir occasionally until butter turn into brown color.
3. Add heavy cream over butter and mix well with wooden spoon.
4. Add brown sweetener and let it simmer on low heat for 4-5 minutes until sweetener is dissolved completely.

The Home Kitchen Ice Cream Cookbook

5. Cook for another 2-3 minutes until sauce thickens but not sticky.

6. Remove from heat and set aside.

7. Meanwhile, mix the cream, coconut extract allulose in small mixing bowl or beat with electric beater until mixture is fluffy.

8. Add shredded coconut in cream mixture.

9. If you are making ice cream without ice cream maker then freeze ice cream container for 24 hours.

10. Pour the mixture into an ice cream container and spoon the caramel sauce and mix well.

11. Freeze for 4 hours or overnight in freezer.

12. Remove ice cream from freezer and serve scoop of ice cream in serving bowl.

13. Drizzle some caramel sauce on top.

14. Serve and enjoy!

NUTRITIONAL INFORMATION

Calories Per Servings, 281 kcal, 26 g Fat, 10 g Total Carbs, 7.6 g Fibre, 2 g Protein

Wilson K. Lee

Peanut Butter Ice Cream

This frozen peanut butter ice cream recipe is perfect for all the nuts in your life! Fold in pecans, peanuts, or chocolate chips to add a pleasant crunch.

Prep Time   10Min

Cooking time 15 Min

Total Time   25 Min

Servings   6

Equipment

Mixing bowl

The Home Kitchen Ice Cream Cookbook

Ice cream container

Ice cream maker.

Cooking Pan

INGREDIENTS

- 1 cup peanut butter
- ½ cup Swerve
- ¼ teaspoon stevia extract powder
- ¼ teaspoon monk fruit powder optional
- ¼ cup natural whey protein
- ⅛ teaspoon salt
- 1 cup unsweetened almond milk
- 1 ⅓ cups heavy cream
- ¼ teaspoon xanthan gum
- 2 teaspoons vanilla extract
- 4 oz. pecans

DIRECTIONS

1. Mix peanut butter with sweetener, whey protein, and salt in large mixing bowl.
2. Add almond milk and xanthan gum in peanut butter mixture.
3. Now add heavy cream, vanilla extract and pecans.

Wilson K. Lee

4. If you are making ice cream without ice cream maker then freeze ice cream container for 24 hours.
5. Pour mixture into ice cream maker and process until churn.
6. Alternatively, pour mixture in container and freeze for 4 hours.
7. Remove ice cream from freezer and serve scoops in serving bowl.
8. Serve and enjoy!

NUTRITIONAL INFORMATION

Calories Per Servings, 240 kcal, 18 g Fat, 13 g Total Carbs, 7.6 g Fibre, 4 g Protein,

The Home Kitchen Ice Cream Cookbook

Almond Butter Ice Cream

Peanut allergy? This Almond butter low carb ice cream is loaded with chopped almonds and cashew is fluffy and creamy, sugar free and for the people who want to reduce weight or diet conscious.

Prep Time   15 Min

Servings   6

Equipment

Mixing bowl

Ice cream container

Wilson K. Lee

Ice cream maker.

Cooking Pan

INGREDIENTS

- 1-½ cup almond milk, vanilla or other flavors
- 1 cup almond butter, unsalted
- 1 teaspoon vanilla extract
- ½ cup coconut oil
- ⅓ cup maple flavored syrup
- 1 oz. chopped almonds
- 1 oz. chopped cashew

DIRECTIONS

1. Add all recipe ingredients blender except chopped almonds and cashew.
2. Blend until all ingredients are mix well.
3. Carefully fold in chopped almonds and cashew.
4. If you are making ice cream without ice cream maker then freeze ice cream container for 24 hours.
5. Pour mixture into ice cream maker and process until churn.
6. Alternatively, pour mixture in container and freeze for 4 hours.

The Home Kitchen Ice Cream Cookbook

7. Remove ice cream from freezer and serve scoops in serving bowl.

8. Drizzle chopped nuts on top and enjoy!

NUTRITIONAL INFORMATION

Calories Per Servings, 486 kcal, 49 g Fat, 13 g Total Carbs, 7.6 g Fibre, 1 g Protein

Wilson K. Lee

Pumpkin Ice Cream

This festive fall classic is made with coconut milk, pumpkin puree and other spices and without any ice cream machine! Delicious served with apple cider or pie.

Prep Time   10Min

Cooking time 15 Min

Total Time   25 Min

Servings   6

Equipment

Mixing bowl

The Home Kitchen Ice Cream Cookbook

Ice cream container

Ice cream maker.

Cooking Pan

INGREDIENTS

- 3 1/4 cup coconut milk
- 1 cup pumpkin puree
- 3 tbsp vodka
- 1/2 tsp cinnamon
- 1/4 tsp allspice
- 1/4 tsp cardamon
- 1/4 tsp cloves
- 1/4 tsp ginger
- 6 tbsp powdered erythritol
- 1/2 tsp stevia extract powder
- 1/2 tsp xanthan gum
- 5 egg yolks
- 1 oz. roasted pumpkin seeds

DIRECTIONS

Wilson K. Lee

1. Add milk, pumpkin puree, vodka, cinnamon, allspice, cardamon, cloves, ginger, powder erythritol, stevia extract in cooking pan and put on medium heat.
2. Cook and stir until mixture bring to boil.
3. Remove from heat and set aside.
4. Beat egg yolks in small bowl and add some mixture in it.
5. Add this in rest of the mixture and mix well until there is no lump.
6. Let the mixture stand on room temperature for 1 hour.
7. Strainer mixture with strainer and remove and solids.
8. If you are making ice cream without ice cream maker then freeze ice cream container for 24 hours.
9. Pour mixture into ice cream maker and process until churn.
10. Alternatively, pour mixture in container and freeze for 4 hours.
11. Remove ice cream from freezer and serve scoops in serving bowl.
12. Drizzle roasted pumpkin seeds on top and enjoy!

NUTRITIONAL INFORMATION

Calories Per Servings, 153 kcal, 9 g Fat, 10 g Total Carbs, 7.6 g Fibre, 7 g Protein

Cashew Butter Ice Cream

Cashews are such an underrated source of protein! This recipe is made with cashew butter, cashew, cream and other ingredients and without any ice cream machine.

Prep Time   15 Min

Servings   6

Equipment

Mixing bowl

Ice cream container

Wilson K. Lee

Ice cream maker.

Cooking Pan

INGREDIENTS

- 1 cup cashew chopped
- 2 tablespoons lemon juice
- 1 tablespoon water
- 1/8 teaspoon cashew extract
- 1/4 teaspoon vanilla extract
- 1/8 teaspoon stevia
- 1 1/2 cups cashew cream
- 1 1/8 cups cashew butter
- 1/3 cup low carb sugar
- 2 tablespoons vanilla flavored vodka
- 1/4 teaspoon salt
- 1/2 teaspoon stevia glycerite

DIRECTIONS

1. Pour all ingredients in blender and blend to make a smooth paste.
2. If you are making ice cream without ice cream maker then freeze ice cream container for 24 hours.

The Home Kitchen Ice Cream Cookbook

3. Pour mixture in Ice cream container and freeze for 4-6 hours until set.

4. Serve scoops of ice cream in bowl with cashew on top.

5. Enjoy!

NUTRITIONAL INFORMATION

Calories Per Servings, 528 kcal, 68 g Fat, 16 g Total Carbs, 7.6 g Fibre, 9.59 g Protein

Wilson K. Lee

Avocado Cream Cheese Ice Cream

This summer creamy recipe is the perfect combo of avocado and chocolate for the superfood lovers and flavor adventurers. And sugar free at that!

Prep Time   15 Min

Servings   6

Equipment

Mixing bowl

The Home Kitchen Ice Cream Cookbook

Ice cream container

Ice cream maker.

Cooking Pan

INGREDIENTS

- 2 ripe small avocados, peeled and pitted
- ½ cup heavy cream or full fat coconut milk
- 1 cup cream cheese
- 2 tbsp coconut oil, melted
- 2 oz sugar free chocolate, chopped and melted
- 2 tbsp cocoa powder
- ¼ cup or to taste granulated Stevia
- 1 tsp vanilla extract
- pinch of salt

DIRECTIONS

1. Blend avocado, heavy cream, cream cheese and coconut oil in a high-speed blender and blend until all ingredients are well incorporated.
2. Add melted chocolate, cocoa powder, sweetener, and vanilla extract and blend again for 2-3 minutes until mixture is smooth and creamy.

Wilson K. Lee

3. If you are making ice cream without ice cream maker then freeze ice cream container for 24 hours.
4. Spoon mixture into ice cream maker and process until churn.
5. Alternatively, pour mixture in container and freeze for 4 hours.
6. Remove ice cream from freezer once ice cream is set.
7. Scoop with an ice cream scoop and serve.
8. Enjoy!

NUTRITIONAL INFORMATION

Calories Per Servings, 433 kcal, 17.93 g Fat, 63.99 g Total Carbs, 7.6 g Fibre, 9.59 g Protein

The Home Kitchen Ice Cream Cookbook

Lemon Curd Pie Ice Cream

Lemon curd is a delicious, tart treat great on toast, or in pies, but most importantly —this ice cream! It's also super easy to make if you don't have any on hand. Just four ingredients plus optional vodka, you're in for a fun quick treat!

Prep Time   15 Min

Servings   6

Equipment

Mixing bowl

Wilson K. Lee

Ice cream container

Ice cream maker.

Cooking Pan

INGREDIENTS

- 1 1/2 cup heavy whipping cream
- 1/3 cup powdered Swerve Sweetener
- 1 cup Lemon Curd chilled
- 2 tbsp vodka optional
- 1 tsp. lemon zest

DIRECTIONS

1. Mix and beat cream, powdered Swerve, and lemon curd in bowl with beater until well combined. Add in vodka and mix again.
2. If you are making ice cream without ice cream maker then freeze ice cream container for 24 hours.
3. Pour mixture in ice cream container and freeze for 4-6 hours.
4. Serve scoop of ice cream with lemon zest on top.
5. Enjoy!

NUTRITIONAL INFORMATION

The Home Kitchen Ice Cream Cookbook

Calories Per Servings, 113 kcal, 11 g Fat, 3 g Total Carbs, 7.6 g Fibre, 1 g Protein

Wilson K. Lee

Strawberry Cheesecake Ice cream

The perfect combo of all your favorite desserts: Ice Cream, Cheesecake, and Strawberry shortcake. This recipe calls for strawberries, cream cheese, and is made without any ice cream machine.

Prep Time   15 Min

Servings   6

Equipment

Mixing bowl

The Home Kitchen Ice Cream Cookbook

Ice cream container

Ice cream maker.

Cooking Pan

INGREDIENTS

- 1 can coconut cream
- 8 oz. cream cheese
- 1/2 cup Sweetener
- 1 tsp vanilla extract
- 1/4 tsp xanthan gum
- 1/2 cup diced strawberries

DIRECTIONS

1. Beat coconut cream and cream cheese in a bowl and with electric beater until cream in chunky and fluffy.
2. Add the swerve, vanilla, and xanthan gum in cream mixture and mix well.
3. Blend strawberries in blender on high speed.
4. Carefully fold in strawberry in cream cheese mixture.
5. If you are making ice cream without ice cream maker then freeze ice cream container for 24 hours.
6. Pour mixture in ice cream container and freeze for 4-6 hours.

Wilson K. Lee

- Serve scoop of ice cream with fresh strawberries on top.
- Enjoy!

NUTRITIONAL INFORMATION

Calories Per Servings, 381 kcal, 38 g Fat, 7 g Total Carbs, 7.6 g Fibre, 5.67 g Protein

Keto Coconut Ice Cream

This easy to make low-carb, sugar-free, Keto Coconut Ice Cream is gluten free and egg free. This creamy recipe is made without an ice cream maker using coconut milk, coconut flour and heavy whipped cream.

Prep Time   15 Min

Servings   10

Equipment

Mixing bowl

Wilson K. Lee

Ice cream container

Ice cream maker.

Cooking Pan

INGREDIENTS

- 4 cups Coconut milk
- 2 cups Whipping Cream
- 1 cup sugar substitute
- 1tsp xanthan gum
- 1 tbsp. Glycerine
- 2 oz. coconut flour
- Coconut slice for topping

DIRECTIONS

1. Beat whipping cream with sweetener in small mixing bowl until fluffy.
2. Add rest of the ingredients and mix well.
3. If you are making ice cream without ice cream maker then freeze ice cream container for 24 hours.
4. Pour mixture in ice cream container and freeze for 4-8 hour until set and firm.
5. Serve ice cream scoop in bowl with coconut slice on top.

The Home Kitchen Ice Cream Cookbook

6. Enjoy!

NUTRITIONAL INFORMATION

Calories Per Servings, 134 kcal, 5.91 g Fat, 7.12 g Total Carbs, 7.6 g Fibre, 3.65 g Protein

Chapter 6 - Granita Recipes

Watermelon Granita

This Watermelon Granita recipe is made with three simple ingredients and is a super delicious, refreshing and quick treat in hot weather. You can make this recipe in advance and can store in freezer up to 2 weeks.

Prep Time   15 Min

Servings   4

The Home Kitchen Ice Cream Cookbook

Equipment

Mixing bowl

Ice cream container

Ice cream maker.

Cooking Pan

INGREDIENTS

- ½ medium seedless watermelon
- 1 tbsp lime juice
- ¼ cup sugar

DIRECTIONS

1. In a blender or food processor, blend watermelon until it becomes puree.
2. It will make or extract about 6 cups watermelon juice.
3. Strain puree with strainer and press with spoon to extract all juice.
4. Discard seeds and pulp of water melon.
5. Add lime juice and sugar in water melon juice, mix well until sugar is dissolved completed with juice.
6. If you are making ice cream without ice cream maker then freeze ice cream container for 24 hours.

Wilson K. Lee

7. Pour juice in large baking dish or container and freeze for about 2 hours.

8. Remove container from freezer and scrape frozen juice with fork and freeze again.

9. Repeat this step after 1 hour for 5-6 times until all mixture is scraped.

10. Serve in serving glass with watermelon slice and chocolate ice cream on top and enjoy!

NUTRITIONAL INFORMATION

Calories Per Servings, 133 kcal, 17.93 g Fat, 63.99 g Total Carbs, 7.6 g Fibre, 9.59 g Protein

The Home Kitchen Ice Cream Cookbook

Mango-Lime Granita

This Mango Lime granita recipe is also made from just three simple and fresh ingredients. The flavors of lime and mango will transfer you to a tropical destination no matter where you live.

Prep Time   15 Min

Servings   4

Equipment

Wilson K. Lee

Mixing bowl

Ice cream container

Ice cream maker.

Cooking Pan

INGREDIENTS

- 3 cups chopped ripe mango
- 1 cup water
- Juice of 2 limes
- 2 tablespoons sugar

DIRECTIONS

1. In a blender or food processor, blend mango until it becomes puree.
2. Add water lime juice and sugar, blend again.
3. Strain puree with strainer and press with spoon to extract all juice.
4. If you are making ice cream without ice cream maker then freeze ice cream container for 24 hours.
5. Pour juice in large baking dish or container and freeze for about 2 hours.
6. Remove container from freezer and scrape frozen juice and freeze again.

The Home Kitchen Ice Cream Cookbook

7. Repeat this step after 1 hour for 5-6 times until all mixture is scraped.
8. Serve in serving glass with mint leaves on top and enjoy!

NUTRITIONAL INFORMATION

Calories Per Servings, 175 kcal, 17.93 g Fat, 63.99 g Total Carbs, 7.6 g Fibre, 9.59 g Protein

Wilson K. Lee

Fresh Strawberry Granita

Yet another quick and easy healthy treat! Enjoy in the mornings like a true Italian, or at night with some alcohol for a looser interpretation!

Prep Time   15 Min

Servings   3

Equipment

The Home Kitchen Ice Cream Cookbook

Mixing bowl

Ice cream container

Ice cream maker.

Cooking Pan

INGREDIENTS

1 cup hot water

3/4 cup sugar

2 tablespoons fresh lemon juice

3 cups sliced hulled strawberries

DIRECTIONS

1. In a blender or food processor, blend strawberries with water until it becomes puree.
2. Strain puree with strainer and press with spoon to extract all juice.
3. Discard seeds and pulp of strawberries.
4. Add lime juice and sugar in strawberries juice, mix well until sugar is dissolved completed with juice.
5. If you are making ice cream without ice cream maker then freeze ice cream container for 24 hours.
6. Pour juice in large baking dish or container and freeze for about 2 hours.

Wilson K. Lee

7. Remove container from freezer and scrape frozen juice and freeze again.

8. Repeat this step after 1 hour for 5-6 times until all mixture is scraped.

9. Serve in serving glass with strawberries slice on top and enjoy!

NUTRITIONAL INFORMATION

Calories Per Servings, 123 kcal, 17.93 g Fat, 63.99 g Total Carbs, 7.6 g Fibre, 9.59 g Protein

The Home Kitchen Ice Cream Cookbook

Mint Avocado Granita

Bet you've never had this before! A truly unique treat in texture and flavor. This recipe makes for a great palette cleanser between courses or refeshing morning snack!

Prep Time   15 Min

Servings   4

Equipment

Wilson K. Lee

Mixing bowl

Ice cream container

Ice cream maker.

Cooking Pan

INGREDIENTS

- 1-1/2 cups coconut water
- 1 avocado, pitted and peeled
- 1/2 peach, peeled
- 3 tablespoons maple syrup
- 1 bunch mint leaves
- 1 tablespoon ginger liqueur
- 1 lime, zest and juice

DIRECTIONS

1. In a blender or food processor, blend avocado mint, coconut water, ginger and peach until it becomes puree.
2. Strain puree with strainer and press with spoon to extract all juice.
3. Discard seeds and pulp of avocado.
4. Add lime juice and maple syrup in juice, mix well until all ingredients are mix well.

The Home Kitchen Ice Cream Cookbook

5. If you are making ice cream without ice cream maker then freeze ice cream container for 24 hours.

6. Pour juice in large baking dish or container and freeze for about 2 hours.

7. Remove container from freezer and scrape frozen juice with fork and freeze again.

8. Repeat this step after 1 hour for 5-6 times until all mixture is scraped.

9. Serve with mint leaves on top and enjoy!

NUTRITIONAL INFORMATION

Calories Per Servings, 150 kcal, 17.93 g Fat, 63.99 g Total Carbs, 7.6 g Fibre, 9.59 g Protein

Wilson K. Lee

Coconut Raspberry Granita

With just 5 natural ingredients, you can't go wrong with this granita recipe bursting with tart and tropical flavors to be enjoyed any time of day.

Prep Time   15 Min

Servings   4

Equipment

Mixing bowl

The Home Kitchen Ice Cream Cookbook

Ice cream container

Ice cream maker.

Cooking Pan

INGREDIENTS

- 1-1/2 cups coconut water
- 3 tablespoons maple syrup
- 1 bunch mint leaves
- 4 cups fresh raspberries
- 1 lime, zest and juice

DIRECTIONS

1. In a blender or food processor, blend raspberries, coconut water until it becomes puree.
2. Strain puree with strainer and press with spoon to extract all juice.
3. Discard seeds and pulp of raspberries
4. Add lime juice and maple syrup in juice, mix well until all ingredients are mix well.
5. If you are making ice cream without ice cream maker then freeze ice cream container for 24 hours.
6. Pour juice in large baking dish or container and freeze for about 2 hours.

Wilson K. Lee

7. Remove container from freezer and scrape frozen juice with fork and freeze again.

8. Repeat this step after 1 hour for 5-6 times until all mixture is scraped.

9. Serve and enjoy!

NUTRITIONAL INFORMATION

Calories Per Servings, 114 kcal, 17.93 g Fat, 63.99 g Total Carbs, 7.6 g Fibre, 9.59 g Protein,

The Home Kitchen Ice Cream Cookbook

CALORIES IN FOOD: CALORIE

CHART DATABASE

Food Categories	Measure	Calories
MILK PRODUCTS		
Whole Milk	225 ml (1 cup)	150
Paneer (Whole Milk)	60 gms	150
Butter	1 tbsp	45
Ghee	1 tbsp	45
FRUITS		
Apple	1 small	50 - 60
Banana	1/2 medium	50 - 60
Grapes	15 small	50 - 60
Mango	1/2 small	50 - 60
Musambi	1 medium	50 - 60
Orange	1 medium	50 - 60
CEREALS		
Cooked Cereal	1/2 cup	80
Rice Cooked	25 gms	80
Chapatti	1 medium	80
STARCHY VEGETABLES		
Potato	1 medium	80
Dal	1 large katori	80
Mixed Vegetables	150 gms	80

Wilson K. Lee

PROTEIN / MEAT		
Fish	50 gms	55
Mutton	1 oz	75
Egg	1 item	75
Cooked Food		
Biscuit (Sweet)	15 gms	70
Cake (Plain)	50 gms	135
Cake (Rich Chocolate)	50 gms	225
Dosa (Plain)	1 medium	135
Dosa (Masala)	1 medium	250
Pakoras	50 gms	175
Puri	1 large	85
Samosa	1 piece	140
Vada (Medu)	1 small	70
MAIN DISHES		
Biryani (Mutton)	1 cup	225
Biryani (Veg.)	1 cup	200
Curry (Chicken)	100 gms	225
Curry (Veg.)	100 gms	130
Fried Fish	85 gms	140
Pulav (Veg.)	100 gms	130
SWEET DISHES		
Carrot Halwa	45 gms	165
Jalebi	20gms	100
Kheer	100 gms	180
Rasgulla	50 gms	140

The Home Kitchen Ice Cream Cookbook

BEVERAGES		
Beer	125 fl. oz	150
Cola	200 ml	90
Wine	3.5 fl. oz	85

Wilson K. Lee

COOKING MEASUREMENT

(CONVERSIONS)

CUPS		
1 cup flour	4oz.	110g
1 cup sugar (crystal or castor)	8oz.	230g
1 cup icing sugar (free of lumps)	5oz.	140g
1 cup shortening (butter, marg. etc.)	8oz.	230g
1 cup honey, golden syrup, treacle	10oz.	280g
1 cup brown sugar (lightly packed)	4oz.	110g
1 cup brown sugar (firmly packed)	5oz.	140g
1 cup soft breadcrumbs	2oz.	60g
1 cup dry packet breadcrumbs	4oz.	110g
1 cup rice (uncooked)	6oz.	170g
1 cup rice (cooked)	5oz.	140g
1 cup mixed fruit (sultanas etc.)	4oz.	110g
1 cup grated cheese	4oz.	110g
1 cup nuts (chopped)	4oz.	110g

The Home Kitchen Ice Cream Cookbook

1 cup coconut	2½oz.	71g

SPOONS (LEVEL TABLESPOONS)

1 oz. flour	2	
1 oz. sugar (crystal or castor)	1½	
1 oz. icing sugar (free from lumps)	2	
1 oz. shortening	1	
1oz. honey	1	
1oz. gelatin	2	
1oz. cocoa	3	
1oz. corn flour	2½	
1oz. custard powder	2½	

LIQUID

1 cup liquid	8oz.	230mls.
21/2 cups liquid	20oz.(1 pint)	575mls.
4 cups liquid	32oz.	1 liter
2 tablespoons liquid	1oz.	30mls.
1 gill liquid	5oz.(1/4 pint)	150mls.

METRIC

Wilson K. Lee

cup measures listed use the 8 liquid ounce cup

spoon measures listed are ordinary household cutlery

2 teaspoons = 1 dessertspoon

2 dessertspoons = 1 tablespoon

4 teaspoons = 1 tablespoon

1 ounce = 28.352 gram. (for convenience work on 30grams)

1 lbs. = 453 grams <> 2.2 lbs. = 1Kg

2 pounds 3 ounces = 1 kilogram

The Home Kitchen Ice Cream Cookbook

CONCLUSION

There you have it! The complete guide to crafting quality frozen desserts from home. With over 90+ recipes, you're sure to have a sweet treat for practically any occasion.

We've covered the most common issues that home ice cream makers encounter like texture and consistency, and the quick and easy ways to solve them so you can catch mistakes before they're made. We also talked about all the incredible benefits of making frozen desserts at home like having full control, knowledge, and customizability of the ingredients you're feeding your friends and family. Hopefully the Tips & Tricks sections gave you all the information and confidence you needed to churn out tons of top-notch treats.

By including the best possible variety of recipes, there's sure to be something for all the people in your life. After all, everyone deserves to enjoy delicious frozen treats regardless of dietary restrictions like Keto, carbohydrate restrictions, and vegan lifestyles! Our recipes with fresh, unique flavor combinations are sure to keep your friends or customers always on their toes, while the classic favorites give them something to come back for again and again. No matter what, this book is a crowd pleaser!

Undoubtedly, your friends and family are thoroughly enjoying every last lick. We're sure you've gotten loads of questions

Wilson K. Lee

about how you could've possibly crafted such delicious ice cream from scratch, and we're happy to share! This book makes a great gift for any ice cream lover in your life, but if you'd rather take all the credit, we can keep a secret too.

If by chance you've uncovered a passion for crafting frozen treats and are ready to take the next step and follow your dreams, this book is a great foundation for building your own home kitchen or storefront small business menu! For more great resources on how to build, own, and operate your own food or beverage business check out my website, wilsonklee.com or my YouTube channel at Wilson K Lee. There you'll find tons of articles, videos, and guides to turning your great concept into a profitable business reality.

No matter your experience or future with ice cream I sincerely hope this book brought you lots of frozen fun!

- Wilson

Manufactured by Amazon.ca
Bolton, ON